D1617540

POLITICS OF AGRICULTURAL CO-OPERATIVISM

This book is a detailed analysis of the evolution of state-sponsored agricultural co-operativism in Peru, an Andean country with high levels of land concentration and widespread rural poverty. Most Peruvian agricultural co-operatives were organized during the military populist government of Velasco Alvarado which, after radical land reform, transformed expropriated estates into co-operatives. From the start, these projects became subject to multiple pressures which ranged from unfavourable government economic policies — designed to promote import-substitution industrialization at the expense of the agricultural sector — to the growth of the co-operative bureaucracy and the deterioration of labour discipline.

A shift toward market-oriented economic strategies after the fall of the Velasco government aggravated the co-operatives' difficulties. Stabilization programs implemented by Velasco's successor, General Morales Bermudez, and liberalization of the national economy by the civilian government of Belaunder Terry dealt a severe blow to Peru's co-operative agriculture. The ensuing crisis gave rise to political mobilization against the market-oriented economic policies. However, the effectiveness of this movement was undermined by a trend toward dissolution of agricultural co-operatives by many members who turned to individual/private agriculture as a solution. Korovkin examines not only the diverging responses of co-operative members to the crisis, but also the external policy-related and internal organizational causes behind it.

The focus of the book is on the cotton-growing sector which constituted the backbone of the state-sponsored co-operative movement in Peru. The analysis of the national dynamic is complemented by case studies of three cotton estates converted into agricultural production co-operatives. One of these proved reasonably successful, while the other two experienced serious economic difficulties, looking for their solution either in political mobilization against the government's economic policies or in the shift to individual/private agriculture. The comparative analysis of their experiences provides valuable insights into the nature of organizational problems confronting Peru's co-operative movement.

Korovkin also places the discussion of the Peruvian co-operative experience in a broader historical and theoretical perspective, focusing on the changing nature of social alliances and economic strategies during the populist and post-populist periods.

Politics of Agricultural Co-operativism is the second in a series of books on academic subjects dealing with Latin America and the Caribbean. It is a co-publication of UBC Press and the Centre for Research on Latin America and the Caribbean (CERLAC).

TANYA KOROVKIN is an assistant professor in the political science department at the University of Waterloo and a fellow of the Centre for Research on Latin America and the Caribbean.

Politics of Agricultural Co-Operativism:

Peru, 1969-1983

Tanya Korovkin

University of British Columbia Press
Vancouver

ISBN 0-7748-0349-5

Canadian Cataloguing in Publication Data
Korovkin, Tanya
    Politics of agricultural co-operativism:
Peru, 1969-1983
    Published in association with the Centre for
Research on Latin America and the Caribbean.
    Includes bibliographical references.
    ISBN 0-7748-0349-5

    1. Agriculture, Co-operative – Peru – His-
tory – 20th century. 2. Agriculture and state –
Peru. 3. Peru – Politics and government – 1968 –
I. York University (Toronto, Ont.). Centre for
Research on Latin America and the Caribbean.
II. Title.
HD1491.P4K67 1990   334'.683'0985
C90-091228-6

This book has been published with the help of a
grant from the Social Science Federation of Canada, using funds provided by the Social Sciences and Humanities Research Council of
Canada.

UBC Press
6344 Memorial Rd
Vancouver, B.C. V6T 1W5

To my mother

Contents

TABLES

Abbreviations

APRA Alianza Popular Revolucionaria Americana/American Popular Revolutionary Alliance

CAP Co-operativa Agraria de Producción/Agricultural Production Co-Operative

CCP Confederación Campesina del Perú/Peruvian Peasant Confederation

CEDEP Centro de Estudios para el Desarrollo y la Participación/Centre of Research for Development and Participation

CENCIRA Centro Nacional de Capacitación e Investigación para la Reforma Agraria/National Centre for Agrarian Reform Training and Research

CGTP Confederación General de Trabajadores del Perú/General Confederation of Peruvian Workers

CNA Confederación Nacional Agraria/National Agrarian Confederation

COCOP Comité para la Coordinacion de Organizaciones Populares/Committee for Coordination of Popular Organizations

ENCI Empresa Nacional de Comercialización de Insumos/National Entreprise for Marketing of Inputs

EPCHAP Empresa Pública de Comercialización de Harina de Pescado/Public Entreprise for Marketing of Fishmeal

EPSA Empresa Pública de Servicios Agropecuarios/Public Entreprise for Agricultural Services

FENCAP Federación Nacional de Campesinos del Perú/National Federation of Peruvian Peasants

FRADEPT Federación Agraria Departamental de Piura y Tumbes/Departmental Agrarian Federation of Piura and Tumbes

ONA Organización Nacional Agraria/National Agrarian Organization

ONDECOOP Oficina Nacional de Desarrollo Cooperativo/National Office for Co-Operative Development

PSR Partido Socialista Revolucionario/Socialist Revolutionary Party

SAF-CAP Sistema de Apoyo y Fiscalización de las Cooperativas Agrarias de Producción/System for Assisting and Auditing Agricultural Production Co-Operatives

SINAMOS Sistema Nacional de Apoyo a la Movilización Social/National System of Support for Social Mobilization

SNA Sociedad Nacional Agraria/National Agricultural Society

Preface

The early 1980s in Peru witnessed apparently contradictory political events. The return to civilian rule after twelve years of military dictatorship opened vast possibilities for popular political participation. These possibilities, however, were not always fully used: the transition to democracy was accompanied by a partial retreat (*reflujo*) in popular mobilization. The situation was especially curious for the agricultural co-operative movement. It emerged from military rule as a national political force representing the agricultural co-operatives. Under the civilian government of Fernando Belaunde Terry (1980-85), the co-operative movement involved itself in a series of national events — strikes, demonstrations, and congresses — which demonstrated its considerable political strength. At the same time, however, the movement was undermined from within by the dissolution of its organizational bases. Increasingly, agricultural production co-operatives (the core of the co-operative sector) subdivided their lands between members and switched to small-scale agriculture. By the mid-1980s, this process reached catastrophic proportions, threatening the very existence of the agricultural co-operative movement outwardly so active in the national political arena. How can this apparent contradiction be explained?

The immediate cause of both the political mobilization and the disintegration of the co-operative sector seemed to lie in the economic crisis affecting co-operative agriculture as the decade began. This economic crisis was related to the Belaunde government's attempts to liberalize the national economy, which had been placed under state controls during the early years of military rule. The change in national economic policies, however, could hardly be the only reason for the co-operatives' economic difficulties. Internal organizational problems also seemed to be important. The studies of agricultural co-operatives in Latin America suggest that co-operatives have been frequently plagued by mismanagement and internal conflicts. If this was also true in Peru (as it seemed to be), what factors accounted for these problems? How did they generate the centrifugal forces responsible for the eventual dissolution of many production co-operatives? And why did these forces develop in some co-operatives but not in others? After all, while some production co-operatives were falling apart, others were mobilizing politically in defence of co-operative agriculture.

This book attempts to answer these questions on the basis of field research conducted in Peru in 1982 and 1983. It could not have been completed without generous assistance from many institutions and persons. Financial support for my research was provided by the Social Sciences and Humanities Research Council of Canada (SSHRCC). My greatest intellectual debt is to Liisa North, Michael Stevenson, and Robert Cox. I also benefitted greatly from discussions with Louis Lefeber, Efraín Gonzales, José Matos Mar, Julio Cotler, Diego García-Sayán, Orlando Plaza, and Heraclio Bonilla.

During my field research, I was a Research Associate in the Department of Social Sciences of the Pontificia Universidad Católica del Perú. I am grateful for the assistance of its faculty and its Chairman, Juan Ossio. I am also greatly endebted to the people working with the National Agrarian Confederation (CNA) and the Peruvian Peasant Confederation (CCP); they provided me with invaluable help in archival and field research. My special thanks go to Pepe Reyes and Raúl Huamán. Without their guidance and judicious advice, this book would not have been written.

In Lima, Leonidas Rodriguez, señora Elena, and don Victor Villanueva together with their family, Tito and Amelia Guiéseckae, and many others helped me in numerous ways, offering introductions and materials for research. In my area of study, I received help from people involved in rural social work and research. I am especially grateful to padre Elmer, Pablo Rondán, and madre Inés. I also wish to thank señora Adelaída and her family, who kindly offered me their friendship and helped me with interviews in the co-operatives. Finally, my most profound debt is owed to the co-operative workers, who let me learn from their experiences.

Politics of Agricultural Co-Operativism

CHAPTER ONE

Introduction

Most students of Third World agricultural co-operatives tend to be highly critical of the co-operatives' economic and social performance. They generally agree that, when compared to universally accepted co-operativist principles, such as democratic management or an equitable distribution of benefits, most Third World co-operatives have been a dismal failure.[1] While critical assessments of co-operatives abound, little effort has been made to relate the problems of their development to social, economic, and political changes taking place in the developing areas. Here, the rise of agricultural co-operativism in Latin America is seen as part of a broader historical change manifested in the transition to capitalist agriculture, the beginning of import-substitution industrialization and the advent of populist politics.

CAPITALIST TRANSITION, LAND REFORM, AND CO-OPERATIVES

Agricultural co-operativism in Latin America developed in a complex social context reflecting the uneven, diverse patterns of transition to capitalist agriculture. At the turn of the century, the Latin American countryside, and the core Andean region in particular (Ecuador, Bolivia, Peru), was characterized by large semi-capitalist estates, or haciendas. Even when most of their agricultural production was destined for the international market, the estates tended to rely on precapitalist forms of labour relations, such as peonage and sharecropping. These estates operated side by side with an independent smallholding sector composed primarily of peasants.[2]

The development of agrarian capitalism increased, not decreased, this social complexity. On many estates, wage relations did not replace peonage and sharecropping altogether, but rather gave rise to mixed or composite forms of labour relations. Moreover, in some cases, the initiative in capitalist modernization was taken by small commercial producers rather than large landowners. Nevertheless, it is generally agreed that the predominant trend in the development of capitalist agriculture in Latin America, at least till recently, has been the capitalist transformation of large estates, a trend frequently described, following Lenin's analysis of Russian agriculture, as a junker road to capitalism.[3]

The junker road in Latin America did not imply the disappearance of the freeholding peasantry; if anything, the peasantry increased in absolute numbers. Its social characteristics, however, changed. Large-scale capitalist agriculture was accompanied by the impoverishment and semi-proletarianization of peasants who became increasingly involved in capitalist production as seasonal wage labourers. Indeed it is frequently argued that peasants in Latin America have become functional to capitalist development. Not only do they continue to supply the growing urban market with cheap food, but they also provide capitalist farmers with cheap seasonal labour. Moreover, the peasant sector is also functional in political terms. According to Stavenhagen (1981b:474-5), it serves as "a buffer zone for millions of underemployed [agricultural] workers who otherwise would die of hunger . . . and who obviously would generate a tremendous pressure upon the social and political system." In a similar vein, de Janvry describes the persistence of the peasant economy in Latin America as functional dualism, a dualism between "the capitalist sector which produces commodities on the basis of hired semi-proletarian labor, and the [impoverished] peasant sector which produces values and petty commodities on the basis of family labor and delivers cheap [seasonal] wage labor to the capitalist sector" (de Janvry 1981:84).

De Janvry's views on the persistence of the impoverished peasantry under capitalism is of particular interest here, because he analyses this phenomenon in relation to land reform, which played an important role in the inception of agricultural co-operatives.[4] According to de Janvry and Ground (1978), land reforms in Latin America tend to accelerate or modify the capitalist transformation of agriculture without changing functional dualism.[5] When land reform is conducted within the semi-capitalist context, it tends to promote the capitalist development of agriculture along the junker road by eliminating precapitalist relations on the haciendas (as was the case in

Bolivia). However, when land reform affects estates having already undergone capitalist transformation, it tends to shift from the junker to the farmer type of capitalist development, manifested in the rise of medium- and small-sized capitalist farms. This happens mostly because large landowners are generally allowed to subdivide their estates to avoid expropriation or, if expropriation actually takes place, they are entitled to a land reserve on the best hacienda lands. De Janvry and Ground suggest that this is what happened in Peru during land reform under the military government of General Juan Velasco Alvarado (1968-75). They are careful to emphasize, however, that in none of the mentioned cases does land reform substantially improve conditions for the freeholding peasantry or eliminate functional dualism. The impoverished peasant sector, in their view, is still "needed" after reform as cheap seasonal labour. In other words, land reforms in Latin America tend to reinforce, rather than reverse, the previous trend of capitalist transformation of agriculture.[6]

Even if de Janvry and Ground are right about the "conservative" impact of land reforms on the relations between the capitalist and peasant sectors, the question remains how these reforms change capitalist and semi-capitalist agriculture affected by the expropriations. This question is not adequately dealt with in their analysis. Focusing almost exclusively on the trend toward structural continuity, they ignore that land reforms can also introduce important changes. Change has been especially pronounced on the estates expropriated under land reform. In many cases, reformist governments attempted to reorganize these estates along generally co-operative lines. These attempts proliferated various types of post-reform agricultural co-operatives, introducing a new structural element into the social make-up of the Latin American countryside. Thus, in Peru, land reform was followed by agricultural production co-operatives whose members owned and worked land collectively. What were the organizational characteristics of these co-operatives?

As stated earlier, the prospects of agricultural co-operativism in the developing areas have generally been treated with much scepticism. One widely accepted conclusion is that, contrary to expectations, it is most unlikely to provide a broad, equitable distribution of the benefits of co-operation among the rural population or to increase rural political participation.[7] Thus, a study conducted by the United Nations Research Institute for Social Development (UNRISD) with the participation of Fals-Borda concludes that "rural cooperatives in developing areas today bring little benefit to the masses of poorer inhabitants. . . . It is the better-off rural inhabitants who mainly take advantage of the cooperative services and facilities, such as government-supported credit and technical assistance channelled through cooperatives" (UNRISD 1975:ix).

In part, this reflects the already noted observation that the semi-proletarianized peasants, constituting the most impoverished social category in the Latin American countryside, tend to be excluded from land redistribution and subsequently organized co-operatives. A co-operative movement created on such a basis would necessarily have a closed, restrictive character, hardly compatible with either the co-operative principle of open membership or the concept of social equity generally associated with co-operativism.

However, the UNRISD conclusions refer not only to the allocation of co-operative benefits among various sectors of the rural population, but also to their distribution inside the co-operatives. In another study sponsored by the UNRISD, Fals-Borda offers ample evidence of intra-co-operative social and economic inequalities. Most importantly, he points to the inefficiency of co-operative democratic institutions (the General Assembly and the Administrative Council), to the predomi-nance of nepotism, and to "a tendency to use the cooperative's resources to benefit personal cliques." All this, in his opinion, contrib-utes to the emergence of the "new *gamonales* [bosses] coming from the cooperative movement" (UNRISD 1971:94).

Fals-Borda's analysis, conducted largely in the modernization per-spective, focuses on cultural-sociological aspects of co-operativism. His major conclusion is that co-operative principles developed in Europe and North America are not suitable for Latin American rural areas because these areas are characterized predominantly by pri-mary forms of solidarity, paternalism, and low-level technical skills (UNRISD 1971:13-14; Fals-Borda 1970:136-7). A different approach to the same problem is adopted by Redclift (1978). He analyses co-operative development in Ecuador in a structural-historical perspec-tive, relating it to the capitalist transformation of agriculture. This transformation, in his opinion, is accelerated and modified by state economic intervention during and after land reform. State policies create the basis for what he calls the institutional differentiation of the peasantry. "As a result of selective capitalist investment by the state and moves to control marketing arrangements, new corporate groups of former tenants [organized in cooperatives] come into being. These corporate groups make short-term economic gains, in some cases, but they simultaneously lose entrepreneurial control over their enter-prises [to the state]" (Redclift 1978:166).

This line of analysis has been developed by Goodman and Redclift (1981) for Latin American co-operatives in general. They emphasize the importance of state-induced forms of transition to capitalist agriculture, which develop not only under land reform, but also as a consequence of the proliferation of state-sponsored technological projects and, generally speaking, of the increased role of the state in promoting agricultural development. Post-reform agricultural co-operatives, in their approach, are institutional devices for channelling state economic assistance to the organized segments of direct producers who, because of this assistance, become co-opted and controlled by the state bureaucracy. Such a situation is likely to create socio-economic differences not only between the co-operative sector and small agricultural producers, but also inside the co-operatives. Some members, especially those occupying the key economic and administrative positions, will be better equipped than the co-operative rank-and-file to capture state-controlled resources.

Goodman's and Redclift's approach is particularly interesting because it provides a historical perspective on the assymetrical relations between the state and agricultural co-operatives, frequently mentioned by students of Latin American co-operativism. Feder (1981), for instance, points out that co-operatives in Latin America frequently become subject to state administrative and political controls. In a similar vein, García writes about a "tendency for the state to substitute for co-operatives in the management of their resources and to replace the democratic administration from the bottom by the bureaucratic one from the top" (García 1976:48). However, while Feder views the state interference with co-operative management in purely negative terms, García suggests that such interference is related to state economic support for co-operative agriculture. This support is essential for the economic "take-off" of the co-operative sector, which otherwise would find itself submerged in a hostile socio-economic environment dominated by private interests.

The state-sponsored co-operative movement, failing to provide for democratic management and an equitable distribution of co-operative benefits, is unlikely to generate a strong co-operativist commitment among its participants. The lack of commitment, can be expected to adversely affect co-operative economic performance. This performance, however, is determined not only by the co-operatives' organizational peculiarities, but also, and most importantly, by government economic policies.

GOVERNMENT ECONOMIC POLICIES AND CO-OPERATIVE AGRICULTURE

Post-reform agricultural policies in Latin America were generally influenced by the import-substitution industrialization (ISI) strategies adopted by nationalist and populist governments in the hope of advancing national economic development. In fact, one main objective of the land reforms resulting in agricultural co-operatives was to promote agricultural production, which had lagged behind a rapidly expanding urban-industrial demand for food and raw materials. The change in the land tenure system was expected to provide a powerful incentive for national agriculture.[8] By and large, however, this expectation failed to materialize. One reason for this failure lies in the peculiarities of intersectoral trade, which benefitted the urban-industrial sector at the expense of the agricultural one.

The intersectoral relations in less developed countries are analysed by Lipton (1974, 1977), who argues that the poor performance of the agricultural sector derives more from the unequal exchange between the urban-industrial and agricultural sectors than from land tenure pattern, although he admits the need for land redistribution in areas of high concentration. According to his analysis, the relations between the two sectors are characterized by "price twists" which discriminate against agricultural producers. These price twists are caused primarily by subsidies for food imports and by price controls on domestically produced foodstuffs. At the same time, locally manufactured goods are overpriced largely because of exchange rate policies designed to protect national industries against foreign competition. Lipton admits that many agricultural inputs, such as fertilizers or machinery, may also be subsidized by governments under agricultural development programs. He argues, however, that these subsidies benefit only a few large commercial farmers (Lipton 1977:287-307).

In political-ideological terms, Lipton feels the poor performance of the agricultural sector is produced by the "urban bias" prevailing among Third World policymakers. This bias, originating in the European intellectual tradition, compels them to allocate resources to the urban-industrial sector, in violation of economic efficiency.[9] Urban bias, described by Lipton as a "state of mind," rests on the convergence of the interests of politically influential groups: both the urban bourgeoisie and urban labour benefit, in different degrees, from low food prices. These groups, identified by Lipton as the "urban class," are opposed by the "rural class" — the rural population suffering from industrial promotion policies (Lipton 1977:13, 63-6).

Lipton has been frequently criticized for his arbitrary, ambiguous definitions of the urban and rural classes, as well as for his failure to grasp the objective, structural underpinnings of intersectoral imbalances in the developing countries.[10] An alternative structural explanation of these imbalances is developed by de Janvry (1981), who analyses them from the dependency perspective. He explains the maintenance of low agricultural prices through the peculiarities of capitalist accumulation in dependent industrializing economies. These economies are characterized by what he calls "social disarticulation": their growth depends on international demand for their exports or the domestic middle- and upper-class demand for sophisticated consumer goods. The role of popular consumption in stimulating expansion in such economies is only marginal. As a result, wage rates under social disarticulation remain low, and so do food prices directly affecting the wage rates. Consequently, the policy of low food prices is a prerequisite for capital accumulation in the dependent economies.

De Janvry's model accounts not only for the preservation of low agricultural prices, but also for government incentives for capitalist agriculture (cheap credit and subsidies for imported inputs also mentioned by Lipton). These incentives are explained by reference to another type of disarticulation characteristic of dependent economies, the "sectoral disarticulation." By this term de Janvry refers to the absence of forward linkages in the production of raw materials and backward linkages in industrial production. Industrialization here implies "external dependency for the import of capital, goods and technology and places equilibrium in the balance of payments as a necessary constraint on the capacity to produce" (de Janvry 1981:33). As a consequence, it requires agricultural development geared toward national food self-sufficiency and increased revenues from exports. But, according to de Janvry, government development efforts concentrate on the capitalist sector responsible for most of the marketable agricultural surplus.

The following chapters show to what extent these generalizations apply to Peruvian agriculture with its sizeable, politically militant co-operative sector. At this point, I would like to note that de Janvry's analysis has dubious empirical validity, because it is conducted largely within the framework of economic determinism. Even if de Janvry admits the importance of political factors in agrarian change, his treatment of these factors remains clearly subordinate to the objective laws of capitalist accumulation. There is little room in his theoretical construct for an analysis of changing patterns of political alliances and social struggles which might directly affect the formulation of economic policies. Actually, policy, in his analysis, assumes a peculiarly static, non-controversial character, invariably serving capitalist accumulation.[11] The analysis of political factors becomes especially important in the case of co-operative agriculture, for, in Peru, at least, it emerged as a state-sponsored alternative to private capitalist agriculture. Moreover, the co-operative movement itself may develop into a political force capable of influencing government economic policies. Below, I discuss changes in the political context of agricultural co-operativism as they relate to changes in both government views on agricultural development and the position of the rural labour force in the national political arena.

CO-OPERATIVES IN THE CHANGING POLITICAL CONTEXT: FROM POPULISM TO POST-POPULISM

Latin American political history has at least two important watersheds. One is the 1929 Great Depression, which dealt a severe blow to Latin American export economies and gave rise to populist movements and regimes committed to ISI. The other is the ISI crisis in the 1960s, which ended the era of populist politics. The post-populist period witnessed the proliferation of repressive authoritarian regimes followed by a sweeping, but not necessarily irreversible, redemocratization.

The upsurge of authoritarianism in the 1960s received particular attention in the literature on Latin America.[12] There is, however, a certain disagreement about its nature and causes. One school of thought, probably best exemplified by Wiarda (1973, 1974a,b), explains it by reference to corporatist values and institutions embedded in the Iberian political culture brought to the New World by Spain and Portugal. The rise of authoritarianism, in this view, demonstrates the strength of corporatist cultural-institutional tradition, which experienced a temporary setback in the 1940s and 1950s, but which prevailed in the subsequent decades.[13]

One of the most interesting studies of corporatism based on Peru under military rule was conducted by Stepan (1978). Contrary to Wiarda, whose definition of corporatism includes a broad range of socio-political characteristics (such as authoritarian and hierarchical patterns of decisionmaking, elitism, and the importance attributed to centralized bureaucracy), Stepan defines corporatism as a system of interest representation regulated or controlled by the state and based on a functional, rather than the partisan/territorial, principle typical of liberal democracies. He argues that corporatist political organization reduces conflict inherent in society and secures the government effective political control.[14]

Stepan agrees with Wiarda that the general principles of corporatism in Latin America have remained unchanged over the centuries. He points out, however, that its historical content may vary. Using Peru under military rule as an example, Stepan distinguishes between "inclusionary" and "exclusionary" corporatism. Inclusionary corporatism is associated with the beginning of ISI and represents an attempt by new state elites to include some popular sectors (mostly urban and rural labour) in the political system reshaped along corporatist lines to reduce the potentially destabilizing impact of popular demands. As a consequence, inclusionary corporatism combines state controls with limited redistributive policies. The immediate outcome is what Stepan calls "co-optative encapsulation" of the popular sectors into state-controlled functional organizations, typical examples of which are the Peruvian agricultural co-operatives created during the Velasco administration (1968-75) (Stepan 1978:73-81).

The political inclusion of the popular sectors gave way to their exclusion after the ISI crisis began. Stepan describes this change as a transition to exclusionary corporatism, which coincides, in Peru, with the overthrow of Velasco and the rise of the repressive government of General Francisco Morales Bermúdez (1975-80). Exclusionary corporatist regimes reduce popular political participation by repression, substituting coercive forms of encapsulation for the previous co-optative ones. They retain some state-controlled functional representative bodies, but lose the redistributive character typical of inclusionary regimes (Stepan 1978:73-81).

The corporatist school offers a perceptive analysis of the historical peculiarities of Latin American political culture and institutions. However, its explanation of the recent upsurge of authoritarianism in Latin America by reference to the corporatist tradition is not entirely satisfactory. To begin with, the concept of corporatism, at least in Wiarda's interpretation, is too broad and vague to accurately analyse political phenomena. Moreover, students of corporatism tend to overemphasize the presumably immutable cultural-institutional underpinnings of Latin American politics and, as a consequence, find it difficult to account for its dynamic quality. Stepan circumvents these problems by offering a rigorous definition of corporatism and distinguishing between its inclusionary and exclusionary types. Nevertheless, his model has only a limited explanatory value. It certainly applies to Peru under military rule. I doubt, however, that it will work equally well for other, more repressive, authoritarian regimes which did not leave much room for any formal interest representation, functional or otherwise. Still, Stepan's distinction between inclusionary and exclusionary politics reflects an important trend in Latin American political history. This trend is analysed from a different angle by O'Donnell (1973, 1977, 1978, 1979) who draws upon the experiences of Brazil, Argentina, Chile, and Uruguay.

O'Donnell relates the rise of authoritarianism in the 1960s to the ISI crisis — a topic which Stepan touched upon, but failed to develop, in his study of corporatism. This crisis, in O'Donnell's view, is caused by exhausting the early stages of ISI, characterized by the production of nondurable consumer goods mostly by domestic industrialists for the middle- and low-income domestic market. In these early stages ISI tends to be associated with populist democracies. They epitomize the trend toward the political and economic inclusion of the worker-popular sectors, manifested in the growth of workers' organizations and improvement in their incomes. At the same time, ISI is conducive to balance-of-payment difficulties arising from a growing gap between the need for imported inputs for domestic industries and the export sector's capacity for generating foreign exchange. These difficulties account for the ISI crisis which led to the rise of authoritarian bureaucratic regimes committed to "deepening" industrialization. By this term, O'Donnell refers to a transition to the production of durable consumer goods for the high-income domestic markets, as well as the production of capital and intermediate goods for domestic industries. This transition involves a massive infusion of foreign capital and technology, which requires co-operation between the national governments and multinational corporations.[15] To create a favourable economic and political climate for multinational corporations, the bureaucratic authoritarian governments suppress worker organizations, dismantle democratic institutions, and eliminate economic gains obtained by organized workers in the earlier stages of ISI. The outcome is political and economic exclusion of the worker-popular sectors incorporated during the populist period.

O'Donnell's analysis of bureaucratic authoritarianism provides an important insight into post-populist politics.[16] However, it poses at least two major problems. First, it is not entirely clear how the political exclusion of the popular sectors is supported by the economic policies adopted by bureaucratic authoritarian regimes. This lack of clarity seems to arise from O'Donnell's emphasis on the perceived need for deepening industrialization by bureaucratic authoritarian regimes, rather than on their actual economic policies. In fact, various authors conclude that most regimes falling into this category (Argentina, Uruguay, Chile) not only fail to advance national industrialization, but do not even consistently pursue this objective. Instead, they rely on a policy mix designed to cope with the immediate problems associated with the ISI crisis: balance-of-payment deficit, inflation, and foreign debt. Generally speaking, these regimes tend to adopt orthodox, market-oriented economic policies (also described as neo-liberal or neo-conservative), which aim at the liberalization of national economies and their closer integration into the world capitalist economy.[17] These policies lower urban and rural popular incomes, and can actually be described as the economic exclusion of the popular sectors. This economic exclusion, however, is not necessarily accompanied by the suppression of formal democratic institutions: the orthodox market-oriented policies in Latin America are implemented by democratic and authoritarian regimes.[18] This brings me to the second problem in O'Donnell's analysis.

O'Donnell suggests that bureaucratic authoritarianism is an almost inevitable outcome of the ISI crisis. In his earlier work, this rather deterministic view was mitigated by describing bureaucratic authoritarianism as a form of political regime analytically separate from the socio-economic structures with which it tends to be associated (O'Donnell 1973). In his later work, however, he forsakes this analytical distinction, defining bureaucratic authoritarianism as a form of state, embodying all the new relations of domination in the post-populist period (O'Donnell 1979). This conceptual extension is criticized by Cardoso, who argues that the notion of the state should refer only to the "basic alliance, the basic 'pact of domination' that exists among dominant classes or fractions of dominant classes," and not specific forms of national political organization (Cardoso 1979:38). It is this alliance, rather than the national political organization, that determines the form of state and conveys the essence of political change in Latin America. Two crucial moments in this process are the rise and fall of developmentalist populism described by Cardoso and Faletto (1979) in their study of dependency and development in Latin America.[19] In their view, the Great Depression and the subsequent industrialization in larger Latin American countries undermined the power of the export (largely landed) oligarchy, giving rise to a populist, or rather, developmentalist-populist alliance. This alliance included the domestic industrial bourgeoisie along with nationalistic sectors of the middle class and counted on the support of urban labour with a stake in ISI. The ISI crisis led to a disintegration of the populist alliance. In the late 1960s and 1970s, it gave way to a post-populist alliance, an alliance of foreign capital and "internationalized" segments of the domestic bourgeoisie with ties to multinational corporations. This realignment caused a shift to market-oriented economic policies, a shift that could take place within both the authoritarian and democratic political frameworks, as the Peruvian case convincingly demonstrates. In fact, Peruvian political experience turns O'Donnell's analysis topsy-turvy, giving support to Cardoso's argument about the need to distinguish between the political regime and the dominant social alliance. In Peru, the economic and political inclusion of the popular sectors took place mostly during the military-populist government of Velasco. However, their economic exclusion, associated with the return to economic orthodoxy, reached its peak under the democratically elected government of Belaunde. The apparent paradox disappears if the focus shifts from the form of political regime to the changes in the dominant social alliance and government economic policies associated with the transition from populism to post-populism. Thus, it can be argued that the Velasco government, acting with a high degree of autonomy from all social classes and groups, attempted to build a developmentalist-populist alliance. By contrast, the Morales rule witnessed an emergence of the post-populist alliance, an alliance of foreign capital and internationalized segments of the domestic bourgeoisie advocating the adoption of market-oriented economic policies. This alliance consolidated its position and completed the shift to economic neo-liberalism after the return to democracy under Belaunde. Thus, contrary to Brazil, Argentina, or Uruguay, where the demise of populism was associated with the collapse of democratic institutions and the rise of authoritarian regimes, in Peru the transition to post-populism started within an authoritarian framework and ended after the return to democracy. The changes in the dominant social alliance and national economic policies involved in this transition, however, showed a considerable similarity in Peru and other Latin American countries.

The focus on the changes in the dominant alliance not only helps to place the Peruvian experiences of military rule in a broader Latin American perspective, but it also sheds light on the evolution of Peru's agrarian politics, providing the key to a better understanding of the changing fortunes of co-operative agriculture. Even though the dominant alliance in Cardoso's analysis tends to be urban-based, it is plausible that in Peru, with its relatively small urban-industrial sector, the agrarian classes and groups play an extremely important role in both populist and post-populist politics. I contend that, contrary to the situation in larger, more industrially developed South American countries, developmentalist populism in Peru appeared mostly in a rural guise. The populist appeal of the Velasco government was directed primarily at peasants and agricultural labourers, not at the industrial workers or the urban poor. Similarly, the centrepiece of his economic and social policies was land reform, without which no successful industrialization was deemed possible. Land reform was followed by agricultural co-operatives seen by the government as the main agent of agricultural development. Under Velasco, co-operatives were granted the economic incentives directed previously to the private sector. As a consequence, co-operative members were generally able to improve their pre-reform standards of living. They were also able to gain at least some access to local and national decisionmaking.

The inclusionary trend was reversed after Velasco's fall. The Morales government suppressed the co-operative movement and withdrew state economic support from the co-operative sector. This led to a crisis in the co-operative economy followed by the dissolution of many co-operatives. Some former co-operative members willingly accepted this dissolution, expecting to become successful capitalist farmers. Others fought back along with other sectors of the population hurt by the swing to economic orthodoxy. These struggles contributed to the collapse of the Morales government and the return to political democracy. However, they did not stop the liberalization of the national economy. The Belaunde government continued dismantling the co-operative sector. The main beneficiaries of its agricultural policies were private capitalists farmers with ties to foreign and domestic agribusiness, who constituted new, influential members in the post-populist alliance.

The following chapters analyse the evolution of Peruvian agricultural co-operativism during the Velasco, Morales, and Belaunde administrations, focussing on the cotton-growing sector. Cotton and sugar cane are Peru's most important export crops, traditionally grown on large land estates (haciendas) situated in fertile coastal valleys. These estates became the first target of the 1969 land reform conducted by Velasco's military government. By the end of his rule, practically all had been tranformed into agricultural production co-operatives. Land reform was welcomed by most cotton workers and tenants who saw an opportunity to gain control of the hacienda lands. The reaction of sugar workers was somewhat different. Unlike the cotton-growing sector, sugar haciendas had a long tradition of trade-unionist struggles led by one of the country's most influential political parties, the American Popular Revolutionary Alliance (APRA). For the *aprista* sugar unions, land reform was little more than a military government's ploy designed to bring the rural labour movement under state control. They accepted the expropriation and co-operativization of sugar haciendas, but resented state interference with co-operative management and refused to join the state-sponsored National Agrarian Confederation (CNA), which represented most of Peru's agricultural co-operatives. Thus, it was primarily cotton co-operatives which took part in the organization of the CNA and subsequently became the pillar of the state-sponsored co-operative movement. And it is these cotton co-operatives that constitute the main objective of my book.

Chapter 2 examines the rise of the co-operative movement as a consequence of the land reform implemented by the Velasco government. I concentrate on the structural characteristics of post-reform production co-operatives and on the relations between the co-operative sector and the state. Chapter 3 deals with co-operative developments under the Morales and Belaunde governments. The focus is on the role of government policies in triggering a co-operative economic crisis and on the contradictory implications of this crisis for the co-operative movement. On the one hand, it led to a co-operative political mobilization against the government's economic policies; on the other, it resulted in the dissolution of many production co-operatives created during the populist period.

In Part Two, I turn to the experiences of three cotton production co-operatives situated in one of the numerous valleys of the Central Coast, Peru's most important cotton-growing region (for reasons of confidentiality, the co-operatives have been given fictitious names). All three were organized in the early 1970s. The estates on which they were formed were quite typical of the Central Coast. They produced mostly cotton, and some food crops. Two depended on wage labour, one practised tenancy. After land reform began, one hacienda was purchased and transformed into a production co-operative by its workers. The other two were expropriated and co-operativized by the government. Given the generally vertical nature of Peru's agricultural co-operativism, these state-sponsored co-operatives were much more representative of the reformed cotton-growing sector than was the independent co-operative organized by its workers. However, given the importance of independent co-operative experiences as a possible alternative to the vertical forms of co-operativism, it seemed justifiable to include it in my analysis along with the two state-sponsored co-operatives. The field work in the co-operatives was conducted in 1982 and 1983. It involved semi-structured interviews and an analysis of archival materials (co-operative accounts and books of records).

Chapter 4 explores the origin and socio-economic organization of the three cotton co-operatives. The focus is on their occupational and income structures, as well as the members' extra-co-operative economic activities designed to complement their co-operative incomes. Chapter 5 examines the co-operatives' political-administrative institutions (the Administrative Council and the General Assembly) as well as their relations with national organizations representing the agricultural co-operative movement. The analysis centers on the nature and implications of bureaucratization which developed in the state-sponsored co-operatives.

In Chapter 6, the co-operatives' economic performance is analysed. In the early 1980s, all three co-operatives plunged into an economic crisis, largely as a consequence of the post-populist change in national economic policies. However, the scope of the crisis varied, depending on the peculiarities of their internal organization as discussed in Chapters 4 and 5. These peculiarities were also responsible for variations in the co-operatives' responses to the crisis. These responses, discussed in Chapter 7, included attempts to exert political pressure on the government through nation-wide political mobilization; internal reorganization designed to reduce production costs without dismantling the production co-operative; and subdivision of co-operative lands leading to the dissolution of the production co-operative.

In Chapter 8, the results of my field work are compared with the results of other studies concerning the development of the agricultural co-operative movement in Peru. I also try to re-evaluate the impact of state intervention on the co-operative movement.

PART ONE: AGRICULTURAL CO-OPERATIVISM: A NATIONAL PERSPECTIVE

CHAPTER TWO

Agricultural Co-Operatives Under Military Populism 1969-1975

In Peru, co-operative agriculture was a product of land reform implemented by the military-populist regime of General Juan Velasco Alvarado. The Velasco government transformed large land estates into agricultural production co-operatives. Their workers and tenants obtained access to land and credit and technical assistance, but they were also placed under state supervision. Operation of the co-operatives was subject to multiple economic and political controls which raised discontent among their members and generated numerous conflicts between the co-operative sector and the state. This chapter discusses the origins and evolution of the Peruvian agricultural co-operativism during the Velasco rule, with special reference to the cotton-growing sector.

LAND REFORM AND THE RISE OF CO-OPERATIVISM

In the 1950s and 1960s, Peru showed clear signs of a junker pattern of transition to capitalist agriculture. The Peruvian countryside was dominated by haciendas   large capitalist or semi-capitalist estates producing export commodities (sugar, cotton, and wool) and, to a lesser extent, foodstuffs for domestic consumption (rice, potatoes, and corn).[1] The haciendas co-existed with a vast sector of independent smallholders, working either on their own (predominant on the coast) or as members of peasant communities particularly numerous in the highland areas, the "Sierra." According to the 1961 national census, as cited in Horton (1976:103), production units over 500 ha (0.5 per cent of the total number) controlled 75 per cent of the farmland while units less than 5 ha (83 per cent of the total number) owned less than 6 per cent. The average unit under 5 ha was actually 1.4 ha, far below what was later considered by land reform officials as the size of an economically viable family unit — 3.5 ha or irrigated land.

The highly skewed pattern of land distribution was complicated by the persistence of precapitalist labour relations, peonage and sharecropping.[2] However, the incidence of these relations was already low by the late 1960s. According to data drawn from the 1961 census, as interpreted by Montoya, the dependent tenants (peons and sharecroppers) constituted only 9 per cent of the total rural labour force. Most rural labourers were independent smallholders (42 per cent), followed by wage earners (31 per cent).[3] These figures indicate that, by the late 1960s, Peruvian agriculture had already reached a relatively high level of capitalist development, manifesting a distinctive functional dualism between the capitalist and the peasant sectors, as described in Chapter 1. The analysis of the evolution of coastal cotton estates offers more evidence in this respect.

In the first third of the twentieth century, the predominant form of production on cotton haciendas was sharecropping, known as *yana-konaje*. In the 1930s and 1940s, the growing political strength of cotton tenants led to a gradual decline of the sharecropping system. Legislation in 1946, which protected the interests of sharecroppers, triggered evictions, followed by the consolidation of cotton haciendas and a progressive spread of direct forms of production. This became more appealing to the large landowners not only because of the new legislation and political mobilization among the tenants, but also because of the cotton boom, which started in the early 1950s and continued into the early 1960s. From 1951 to 1964, the volume of Peruvian cotton exports almost doubled (Eguren 1981:65-6). The swelling revenues from exports permitted large producers to modernize their estates, improving the irrigation infrastructure, increasing the use of agricultural machinery, and substituting wage labour for sharecropping. By the late 1960s, most cotton haciendas had developed into centrally managed capitalist entreprises relying on wage labour.[4]

Centrally managed cotton haciendas were rather complex. They employed a sizeable technical-administrative staff: engineer-agronomists, technicians, bookkeepers, office clerks, and overseers who were practically in charge of the hacienda management. The manual workers fell into two categories: the skilled workers (tractor drivers, mechanics, well operators) and the field workers (whom I also refer to as field labourers). Only a small proportion of field workers, however, was employed permanently as part of the stable hacienda labour force. Most field labourers were hired temporarily even when many worked on the hacienda virtually throughout the year. They were known on cotton haciendas as "permanent temporary" labourers (*los eventuales permanentes*), different from both stable and temporary labourers employed for relatively short periods. In this book I call them quasi-temporary labourers. These quasi-temporary labourers were paid considerably less than stable field labourers. They were also excluded from various social benefits (such as medical and social insurance, free housing) available to the stable labour force. The temporary labourers in the proper sense stood at the very bottom of the hacienda occupational hierarchy. Most were cotton-pickers (*apañadores*) recruited for harvesting primarily among seasonal migrants from the Sierra.[5] By contrast, the quasi-temporary labourers were recruited among local residents. The local supply of temporary and quasi-temporary labour was facilitated by the persistence of the smallholding sector in the cotton areas. In 1972, for example, 66 per cent of all cotton-growing units in three coastal departments (Piura, Lima, and Ica) were less than 5 ha (Eguren 1981:100; Matos Mar et al. 1967; Collin-Delavaud 1967).

In sum, by the time of the military government's land reform in 1969, cotton production in Peru had largely undergone capitalist transformation and had developed two forms of functional dualism. This could be seen in the relations between the capitalist cotton sector (represented most typically by cotton haciendas) and the highland peasant sector which provided them with cheap seasonal labour. It also occurred between the capitalist and the peasant economy in the cotton areas, with the local smallholders employed as quasi-temporary labourers. Generally speaking, these relations remained largely unchanged by land reform.

The 1969 land reform in Peru is generally considered as one of the most radical in Latin America.[6] By July 1976, the government had expropriated and transferred approximately one-fifth of the national farmland (6,810,000 ha) to the new owners (Eguren 1977:227; Instituto Nacional de Planificación 1978:32). The three categories of producers to benefit most from land redistribution were the stable hacienda workers, the dependent tenants, and the independent community peasants (see Table 1). With reference to land transfers, however, the community peasants found themselves at a clear disadvantage as compared to the two other categories. The average transfer per beneficiary for community peasants was only 0.4 standardized ha, while among the dependent tenants it was 2.1 ha, and among the stable agricultural labourers, 3.8 ha.[7] The individual smallholders stood closer to the average land transfers of the stable labourers and depen-

TABLE 1: Social composition of beneficiaries of land reform and average land transfers per beneficiary, Peru, 1979

	%	Average land transfer (in standardized ha)
Stable hacienda workers	27.0	3.8
Dependent tenants	25.3	2.1
Community peasants	38.3	0.4
Individual smallholders	9.4	2.6
Total	100.0	2.0

SOURCE: Caballero and Alvarez 1980:45

dent tenants, but their proportion in the total number of beneficiaries was low in comparison. In cotton areas, where the peasant sector was composed primarily of individual smallholders, land reform benefitted the stable hacienda labourers most. In 1975 in the cotton-growing valley of Cañete, for instance, there were more than 5,000 smallholders who did not benefit from land reform, as compared with 2,900 beneficiaries, mostly stable hacienda labourers (Castillo 1979:38). Similarly, in the cotton-growing department of Piura, land reform benefitted less than 30 per cent of rural families; again, most beneficiaries were stable hacienda workers (Rubín 1977:28-9).

While peasants who were smallholders in cotton areas were largely excluded from land redistribution, neither could they gain much from co-operativization as temporary or quasi-temporary labourers. The membership of cotton production co-operatives was composed primarily of the stable hacienda workers (Harding 1975, Caballero 1978). This situation had far-reaching social and political implications. It triggered land conflicts between the beneficiaries and the non-beneficiaries of land reform, culminating in invasions of co-operative lands by local peasants. It also created strain between the state-sponsored co-operative movement and independent peasant organizations (I will return to these points later).

While leaving functional dualism basically untouched, the 1969 land reform introduced profound changes into the capitalist cotton economy. Its single most important implication was the disappearance of the big agrarian bourgeoisie. The expropriated landowners were entitled to a land reserve under the size limit established by the law. As far as their agricultural activities were concerned (many had also invested in trade, finance, or industry), the landowners were generally transformed into medium agricultural producers, joining the ranks of the small and medium agrarian bourgeoisie which existed prior to land reform. On balance, however, there seemed to be no substantial growth in the number of small and medium capitalist production units. As already mentioned, the expropriated properties by and large became centrally managed co-operatives. At the same time, the Velasco government effectively stopped the private subdivisions which coastal landowners tried to use to avoid expropriations.[8] Further, the expropriations affected many medium-size properties whose owners had been accused of violating labour legislation. In view of these developments, de Janvry's argument about a shift from the junker to the farmer road in Peru after land reform (see Chapter 1) requires certain qualifications. Moreover, the most prominent feature of this reform was the transformation of capitalist and semi-capitalist estates into co-operative production units controlled by the state, which points to the persistence of the junker model in a state-co-operative version.

After the reform, the small and medium agrarian bourgeoisie representing the private capitalist sector in the cotton-growing areas was opposed by the co-operative sector organized from cotton haciendas and composed primarily of agricultural production co-operatives (CAPs). The internal organization of the co-operatives displayed a peculiar mixture of heterogeneous elements, some inherited from the pre-reform haciendas and others introduced through land reform. Legally, the CAP was an indivisible production unit owned and operated collectively by co-operative members, with no individual production within its boundaries. Co-operative members were entitled to a share of co-operative profits paid in proportion to the number of days worked in the co-operative; this was expected to provide for relative equality in members' individual incomes. The supreme authority within the CAP belonged legally to the General Assembly of its members. The Assembly was to make all important administrative decisions, to ratify co-operative production plans and financial accounts, and to elect permanent administrative-representative bodies: the Administrative Council, the Supervisory Council, and a number of special co-operative committees.[9]

The implementation of these regulations, however, was hampered by the peculiarities of cotton production developed in the pre-reform period. Some cotton production co-operatives were organized on haciendas which practised tenancy. Centralizing production in such co-operatives created multiple social problems. The tenants were generally reluctant to hand over their plots to the co-operative and frequently retained them even after becoming co-operative members. As for profit-sharing, it was superimposed on the previously existing wage relations without replacing it. Intraco-operative wage differentials also remained quite pronounced, reflecting the complex hacienda occupational structure. After land reform, this structure remained virtually intact, and wages actually continued to constitute the major source of income among co-operative members.

The occupational continuity was viewed by land reform officials as essential to the economic success of the co-operatives. The economic rationality of their approach seemed to be beyond doubt. However, it soon came into contradiction with the co-operative principle of administration, based on the supreme authority of the General Assembly. This contradiction, aggravated by the persisting difference in incomes, generated multiple intraco-operative conflicts, and conflicts between the co-operative manual workers and the technical-administrative staff, in particular (Harding 1975; Rubín 1977, 1978; McClintock 1981; Montoya 1974).

According to McClintock, who conducted an in-depth study of two agricultural co-operatives on the coast and one livestock co-operative in the Sierra, the contradiction between the co-operative and the occupational principles of management was generally solved in favour of the co-operative. She points to a dramatic increase in worker participation in hacienda management after the organization of co-operatives (McClintock 1981:167-9). By contrast, Rubín, who surveyed cotton and rice co-operatives in the department of Piura, argues that the decisional power of co-operative workers was insignificant, for "the [co-operative] occupational hierarchy provides for the persisting concentration of power . . . in the hands of those who are directly in charge of the operation of a [co-operative] enterprise" (Rubín 1977:52) (Unless otherwise indicated, translations are by the author.)

This divergence of opinions seems to be largely due to the different approaches used by the two authors. McClintock's analysis focuses on the political behaviour of co-operative members and the development of participatory attitudes. The co-operativization of haciendas, viewed thus, certainly implied a considerable change in greater worker participation in decisionmaking. Rubín, by contrast, is more concerned with the organization of co-operative production. She argues that all important co-operative decisions were still made by the professional administrative staff in co-ordination with the state bureaucracy. She admits that the General Assembly played an important role in co-operative life, but indicates that its sphere of influence was mostly limited to the distributional issues previously dealt with by hacienda unions (such as wages, working conditions, social services) and to such apparently radical, but essentially irrelevant, measures as the dismissal of an unpopular manager (Rubín 1977, 1978).

Similar conclusions were reached by other students of Peruvian co-operativism, who emphasized the dominant role played by the co-operative technical-administrative staff and members of state bureaucracies in co-operative decisionmaking (Caballero 1977, 1980; Stepan 1978; Petras and Havens 1981). Caballero, for example, points to the ambivalent nature of the co-operatives created under land reform: they were participatory self-managed bodies pursuing the collective interests of their members, yet state capitalist entreprises, preserving the occupational hierarchy and following the logic of capitalist accumulation under the close supervision of the state (Caballero 1980:89).

In this connection, the role of the state in the administration of cotton co-operatives should be particularly emphasized. For two years after the reform, all agricultural co-operatives formed under Decree-Law 17716 were run by regional Special Administrative Committees composed of officials from the Ministry of Agriculture, the Agrarian Bank, and other government institutions. The state controls became less direct, but no less substantial, after the co-operatives took over their own administration. They still had to submit their annual production plans, payroll, and financial accounts to the Ministry of Agriculture for approval. The Ministry also reserved the right to control wages suggested by the co-operative's General Assembly (prohibiting what it considered to be excessive increases), and to supervise its social spending. The distribution of co-operative profits was also regulated from above. Half had to be transferred into co-operative funds and used for reserves, investment, and other collective needs. Two-thirds of the remaining amount also had to be used for co-operative investment and only what was left could be distributed among co-operative members as their share of profits.[10]

State controls of co-operative administration combined with the preservation of the hacienda occupational hierarchy accounted for a relatively low identification among co-operative members with the co-operative institutions. This led to a progressive deterioration of individual work performance manifested in a number of ways: fewer working hours; employment of a large number of quasi-temporary labourers; multiple infractions of labour discipline; and, finally, illegal appropriation of co-operative property (Caballero 1980).

In sum, the 1969 land reform gave rise to a socially restrictive, bureaucratically structured co-operative movement. The temporary and quasi-temporary labourers in cotton-growing areas were left largely outside co-operativization, which, as I later show, adversely affected relations between their representative organizations and the co-operative movement. At the same time, the co-operatives tended to fall under the sway of the hacienda technical-administrative staff and the state bureaucracy. This explained, to a certain extent, a low

TABLE 2: International cotton prices (in current dollars) and production of cotton fibre, Peru, 1965-75

	1967	1968	1969	1970	1971	1972	1973	1974	1975
PRICES ($ per T)	612	728	651	677	770	826	1,169	1,806	—
PRODUCTION (in 1,000 quintals)	1,927	2,191	1,927	1,989	1,777	1,645	1,773	1,957	1,573

SOURCE: Eguren 1981: Table 5.2 and Appendix 1

commitment among co-operative members to the co-operative institutions, which accounted for their declining individual work performance and subsequent low profitability of the co-operative economy. However, as suggested in Chapter 1, this problem cannot be entirely understood in terms of the internal co-operative organization. It requires an analysis of government post-reform agricultural policies.

AGRICULTURAL POLICIES AND COTTON CO-OPERATIVES

Traditionally, cotton has been one of the most important export crops in Peru. In the early 1950s, it occupied one-third of the total agricultural area on the coast, and in the early 1960s this figure rose to almost one-half (Thorp and Bertram 1978:231). However, by 1968, when Velasco came to power, cotton production in Peru tended to decline. To a large extent, this was caused by the collapse in the early 1960s of the cotton boom which had been fuelled by high world prices. In the 1970s, international cotton prices started rising once again. Nevertheless, the decline continued despite the favourable conjuncture in the international market (see Table 2).

The main reason for this apparent paradox lay in Velasco's ISI policies.[11] In addition to tariff protection, tax exemptions, and credit incentives granted to domestic industries, Velasco established tight controls on exchange rates. The overvalued Peruvian currency facilitated imports of capital goods and foodstuffs needed for the expanding urban-industrial sector. The large and medium cotton producers could benefit from this policy as far as importing agricultural machinery was concerned. However, they also found their revenues from exports considerably curtailed. In 1974, these revenues were reduced even further by the introduction of a 20 per cent tax on agricultural exports. While Velasco's exchange and tax policies penalized cotton growers as exporters,[12] his price control policy affected them as suppliers for the domestic urban-industrial market.

TABLE 3: Average annual domestic consumption and exports of cotton fibre (in 1,000 quintals), Peru, 1967-75

	1967	1968	1969	1970	1971	1972	1973	1974	1975
DOMESTIC CONSUMPTION	323	399	404	487	635	693	683	877	555
EXPORTS	1,530	1,515	1,522	1,455	1,104	1,085	1,021	1,034	795

SOURCE: Eguren 1981: Appendix 1

During the 1960s and early 1970s, cotton was gradually transformed from an export into an industrial crop. By the mid-1970s, more than 40 per cent of the national output was sold in the domestic market (see Table 3).

This trend reflected the growth of the national textile industry — one of the most spectacular successes of the ISI strategy in Peru.[13] To encourage it further, Velasco committed his government to low cotton prices. In 1974, he nationalized the cotton trade, transferring its control to the Public Enterprise for Marketing of Fishmeal and Oil (EPCHAP), a state agency originally engaged in marketing fish products. To a large extent, this measure was dictated by the military's commitment to economic nationalism: in 1970, almost 70 per cent of Peruvian cotton exports was controlled by transnational capital (Eguren 1981:83). It also reflected the regime's concern with expanding the state economic sector in general, and with establishing state controls over foreign trade in particular.[14] In addition, nationalizing the cotton trade enabled the government to fix domestic cotton prices far below the international levels, considerably reducing the costs of domestic textile production. In 1974, when international cotton prices rose approximately one-third over the previous year, the floor prices in constant *soles* paid to domestic cotton producers actually dropped (see Table 4).[15]

The policy of controlled cotton prices under Velasco was part of a more general strategy of price controls designed to protect the interests of the urban-industrial sectors. Long before Velasco came to power, the prices of most foodstuffs in Peru had already been subject to state regulations. Velasco refined this strategy, transferring the marketing of many foodstuffs to the direct control of the state. From 1969 to the end of his rule in 1975, rice, wheat, corn, potatoes — to name just the most important crops — were marketed by the Public Enterprise for Agricultural Services (EPSA), another state agency involved in domestic and foreign trade.

The control of food prices, however, seems to have been more flexible than that of cotton, reflecting the government's commitment

TABLE 4: Average international and domestic Peruvian cotton prices, 1970-75

	International prices (per quintal of Peruvian cotton fibre)	Domestic floor prices (per 1 kg of raw cotton)	
	U.S.$	*soles*	1970 *soles**
1970	33.8	10.554	10.554
1971	40.5	11.574	10.836
1972	43.2	12.199	10.656
1973	62.1	19.392	15.467
1974	93.3	21.091	14.393
1975	71.9	18.799	10.376

SOURCES: Ministerio de Agricultura *Estadística Agraria*, Dec. 1982:Table 24; Portocarrero 1980:Table 18; Salaverry 1982: Table 1.6
*Calculated on the basis of consumer price index used as a substitute for agricultural deflators

to promotional policies for food crops. Nevertheless, the price controls certainly diminished incentives for domestic food production, particularly since they were accompanied by an increased reliance on food imports facilitated by the overvalued *sol*. From 1965 to 1975, the proportion of imported wheat in total domestic consumption grew from 76 to 86 per cent. For corn and sorghum, the increase was from 0 to 52 per cent; for barley, from 10 to 32 per cent (Alvarez 1980:27).[16]

The negative effects of price control policies on domestic agriculture became aggravated in the mid-1970s by the national economic crisis, which marked the end of military populism.[17]

In agriculture, as in industry, the economic crisis manifested itself in soaring production costs. It affected all agricultural producers, but its impact might be expected to be particularly dramatic for co-operative agriculture which, as argued earlier, had already been suffering from deteriorating individual work performance. The Velasco government, however, tried to keep the co-operative sector afloat with generous credit assistance, even though this assistance consisted mostly of short-term loans permitting the co-operatives to cover their annual production expenses, but offering them little or nothing in capitalization. Under Velasco, the co-operative sector enjoyed preferential interest rates unavailable to private producers. The government also considerably expanded the operations of the state-owned Agrarian Bank. From 1970 to 1975, the total amount of state agricultural credit in constant *soles* rose from 7.2 to 9.4 thousand millions (Salaverry 1982:54). Much of it was directed to the co-operatives which had been granted top priority for state agricultural credit. In 1977 (and there are no reasons to believe that the situation was different in 1974 or 1975), production co-operatives received 84 per cent of all state credit for cotton, even though their share in cotton production was considerably lower — only 68 per cent. The situation was similar for other crops. In 1977, rice co-operatives accounted for only 26 per cent of national rice production but received 42 per cent of state rice credit. For corn, the figures were 24 and 51 per cent, and for potatoes 9 and 38 per cent (Alvarez 1980:Table 15).

Financial support for the co-operative sector was complemented by favourable tax policies. Under Velasco's predecessor, Fernando Belaunde Terry, co-operatives had been exempted from a tax on profits paid by private producers. Velasco continued this practice. The effect of this tax incentive on post-reform co-operatives was, however, neutralized by their obligation to pay the agrarian debt under Decree-Law 17716. The transfers involved in the agrarian debt were designed to reimburse the compensation paid by the state to expropriated landowners and, simultaneously, to induce them to invest in industrial development. At the time of expropriation, the landowners were paid the value of their lands and other assets partly in cash and partly in vouchers which they could cash only if they made an industrial investment. However, contrary to the government's expectations, no considerable transfer of capital took place under these provisions, partly because of the procedural confusion surrounding the vouchers and partly because the amount of compensation, calculated on the basis of the book rather than market values, was relatively low (Caballero and Alvarez 980:67-70). While the significance of the agrarian debt in terms of national capital flows was low, it put an additional burden on co-operative finances, draining a considerable part of co-operative profits.

In sum, despite the Velasco government's political commitment to agricultural co-operativism, its economic policies tended to adversely affect the co-operative cotton economy. The price policies designed to promote the national textile industry deprived cotton growers of the benefits of high international prices. Their impact on the cotton economy was later aggravated by soaring production costs due to the national economic crisis. Furthermore, producing largely for export, cotton growers were penalized by government exchange, tax, and credit policies, even though cotton co-operatives were favoured over the private growers for state credit. They also enjoyed tax exemptions unavailable to private producers. However, this advantage was cancelled by their obligation to pay the agrarian debt. Thus, on balance, it seems that the low profitability of co-operative agriculture, at least in the case of cotton, was due not so much to the co-operatives' internal problems as to Velasco's economic policies which were fundamentally adapted to the needs of ISI. These policies were bound to create conflicts between the co-operative sector and the state. The conflicts, however, were likely to remain limited by the terms of the co-operatives' political incorporation, as suggested in Chapter 1. They were also likely to be overshadowed by antagonisms between the co-operatives and the independent peasant organizations questioning the very existence of the post-reform co-operative sector. Below, I examine the political implications of the 1969 land reform, focusing on the peculiarities of the national co-operative movement, as represented by the National Agrarian Confederation (CNA).

CO-OPERATIVISM OR CORPORATISM?

The land reform conducted by the military activated the rural union movement which had grown considerably during the previous decades. The modernization of cotton haciendas was accompanied by the organization of cotton labour unions which integrated stable agricultural labourers. In 1966, there were 123 such unions in Peru, seventy-seven in the department of Lima, thirty-nine in Ica, and 6 in Piura (Cotler and Portocarrero 1969:301). During land reform, the unions played an important role in curbing the resistance of local landowners who frequently succeeded in delaying or totally avoiding expropriations.[18] The union mobilization was accompanied by a growing influence of the political left, represented in the countryside mostly by the Peruvian Peasant Confederation (CCP).[19] Actually, the CCP organized many strikes and land invasions in support of land reform in cotton areas. The CCP, however, insisted not only on the immediate expropriation of cotton haciendas, but also and most importantly, on non-interference by the state in the organization of co-operatives. The CCP looked with suspicion on the government's co-operative activities, seeing in them an attempt to undermine the independent peasant movement. It repudiated the establishment of state controls on co-operative administration and repeatedly called on co-operative members to struggle for co-operative autonomy. In May 1974, the CCP held a national congress which emphasized the importance of developing "the *independent* popular movement, taking advantage of the present struggles between the military and the landowners" (CCP 1974, cited in García-Sayán 1982:Appendix 9, emphasis added). This, however, was not an easy task — at least in the cotton sector. After land reform, cotton labour unions tended to become absorbed by co-operative structures. The union leadership, confronted with a host of administrative problems, showed little interest in political struggles and generally came to terms with the government bureaucrats supervising the co-operative sector.[20]

Losing its influence within the cotton co-operative sector, the CCP increased its presence among those who had been left outside — the smallholders. As already mentioned, land reform primarily benefitted the stable hacienda labourers, frustrating smallholders' hopes of access to hacienda lands. The CCP supported their land claims which were directed against the co-operatives. In cotton-growing areas of Piura, for example, the CCP organized smallholders into Committees of Poor Peasants. In 1974, the committees of Alto Piura invaded more than 2,700 ha of land owned by five local co-operatives. After initial confrontations between the co-operative members and the invaders, a settlement was reached, whereby the invaders were allowed to stay on the disputed lands. They failed, however, to gain access to water for irrigation which continued to be controlled by the co-operatives. Similar incidents, not always peacefully settled, took place in many other areas of the country.[21]

While the reformed sector was literally assaulted by the poor peasants led by the CCP, it also came under attack from the small and medium capitalist producers. After land reform, these relatively privileged producers gained control of an influential organization, the National Agriculture Society (SNA), which traditionally represented the interests of the large landowners. When Velasco prohibited the subdivision of haciendas by private initiative and encouraged the expropriation of smaller estates, the new SNA leadership started a bitter political campaign against land reform. It claimed that the government intended a total elimination of private property, accusing its agencies of "communist infiltration" (Pease 1977:107-11). After several months of bickering, Velasco decided to dissolve the SNA, replacing it by a new rural representative body. In 1972, Decree-Law 194000 dismantled the SNA and created the National Agrarian Confederation (CNA), which was to become the sole legal representative of rural interests. The government's decision to create a new agrarian confederation raised bitter protests among the independent peasant organizations. It is worth remembering, however, that these were not the main target of Velasco's attack. Even if Decree-Law 194000, to use Pásara's expression, "put them legally into brackets," it was directed primarily against the small and medium agrarian bourgeoisie whose interests were represented by the SNA (Pásara 1978:61). Accordingly, the CNA appeared as an alternative not only to the independent peasant movement, but also, and no less importantly, to the organizations of rural propertied classes.

The new CNA formed part of the inclusionary corporatist political framework extensively discussed in the literature on Peru.[22] Its organization was entrusted to a government agency, the National System of Support for Social Mobilization (SINAMOS). In two years, SINAMOS formed 119 provincial Agrarian Leagues and eighteen departmental Agrarian Federations. In 1974, they held their First National Congress, sponsored and financed by the government (CNA 1975a). The CNA's dependence on the state was only too obvious: practically all CNA activities were financed by the government and supervised by appointed advisers. The CNA inevitably sided with the government on controversial political issues and fiercely criticized its opponents (Valderrama 1976:117-18). At the same time, the CNA also sought to expand its own influence within the government. It demanded greater representation in state administrative bodies (it was allowed to send delegates to the Agrarian Bank, EPSA, ENCI, and other agencies dealing with agriculture), as well as modification of some government policies affecting its members. To understand the CNA's demands its social make-up must first be examined.

Presumably, the CNA represented agricultural and livestock co-operatives, peasant communities, associations of smallholders, and associations of landless peasants. The participation of the last two categories, however, was insignificant. According to SINAMOS data cited by McClintock (1983:291), 75 per cent of its membership was drawn from community peasants and 20 per cent from co-operatives.[23] This composition reflected the government's attempt to extend political participation not only to those social sectors which had actually benefitted from land reform (the stable hacienda labourers and tenants), but also to the largely excluded peasantry. In doing so, it hoped to provide them with partial compensation for this exclusion and, at the same time, to counteract the growth of the CCP's political influence. Still, there seems to be little doubt that it was the co-operative sector, and not the community peasants, that constituted the hard core of the CNA. Being the major beneficiary of the land reform, the co-operative sector was more willing to support the CNA's initiatives. Moreover, having more economic and organizational resources, it succeeded in shaping the CNA's political agenda, focusing on the problems of marketing and agricultural prices, crucial to the reformed sector, rather than on the problem of land, the main concern of the community peasants.

True, the CNA pressed the government for more effective, comprehensive land reform. In the departments of Lima, Ica, Piura, and Cajamarca, it organized strikes and land invasions, demanding the expropriation of estates spared by local land reform agencies. However, the continuing peasant demands for land put the CNA into a difficult situation. These demands could be partially met by lowering the ceiling on landed property — to which the CNA did not object. This, however, would hardly satisfy the discontented peasants whose claims were centred on the former hacienda lands transferred to co-operatives. The CNA categorically rejected these claims, viewing them as a CCP-inspired political machination designed to destroy the co-operative sector (CNA 1974).

While the question of land had a highly divisive effect on the CCP and the CNA (already quite hostile because of the privileged political status of the latter), the questions of marketing and agricultural prices offered some grounds for co-operation. Moreover, they provoked the first disagreement between the CNA and the military government, making the CNA question, albeit rather timidly, government agricultural policies. When Velasco declared his intention of nationalizing the cotton trade, the Agrarian Leagues representing cotton co-operatives asked for the new system of marketing to be transferred to the control of the direct producers. This would have permitted them to absorb the benefits of the new cotton boom, as well as to prevent domestic cotton prices from falling once the boom was over.

The government, however, was more interested in bringing the revenues from cotton exports into the state treasury, as well as in keeping the domestic prices of cotton sufficiently low to provide the textile industry with a cheap input. Accordingly, it advocated a state monopoly of the cotton trade. Significantly, this controversy united the two rival peasant confederations. In 1974, the cotton-growing peasant community of Catacaos, a member of the CCP, called for a national congress of cotton producers, with the objective of co-ordinating their position on nationalization. The congress was held in Ica, a CNA stronghold, and was attended by 140 delegates from various cotton-growing areas. The congress concluded that the new system of marketing should be controlled by representatives of direct producers (Revesz 1982:133-52). This recommendation was clearly ignored by the government. Several months later, the cotton trade was transferred to EPCHAP, which operated without any meaningful participation by cotton growers — a fact strongly resented by the CNA.

The CNA also tried to intervene in the marketing of food crops (which, incidentally, constituted a sideline of many cotton co-operatives). As already mentioned, the economic crisis of the mid-1970s pushed up agricultural production costs while most farm prices remained subject to state controls. Refraining from questioning state controls as a general policy issue, the CNA concentrated on the promotion of so-called "direct marketing."

Direct marketing involved establishing contacts between agricultural producers and urban consumers, bypassing the traders. In the CNA leadership's opinion, this would improve farm prices without affecting the interests of the urban consumers. An early CNA direct marketing project involved Central Co-operatives — regional units integrating individual co-operatives. Later, the CNA's attempts to increase the co-operatives' participation in marketing was structured around the Committees of Agricultural Producers organized by types of crops (e.g., Cotton Committee, Rice Committee). The new bodies were expected to attain at least two important objectives. First, they could channel state support to individual producers alienated by land reform. Second, they appeared ideal for dealing with the problem of marketing. By organizing all categories of producers according to types of crops, the Committees were designed to establish linkages between both producers and state marketing agencies and between producers and urban consumers.

In 1975, the linkage between producers and urban consumers assumed special importance. The economic crisis had led to food shortages, raising profound discontent among urban low-income groups. To cope with this situation, the CNA founded the Committee for Co-ordination of Popular Organizations (COCOP), integrating various participatory bodies created by the Velasco government. COCOP tried to develop marketing of foodstuffs directly by Committees of Agricultural Producers in co-ordination with shantytown associations. The government's reaction to this initiative was highly negative. A decree issued in July 1975 announced the creation of the so-called System of Agricultural Production under the control of the Ministries of Agriculture and Food to deal with food shortages without the participation of the CNA or other state-sponsored popular organizations.

The controversy around direct marketing was the second major setback in relations between the Velasco government and the CNA, demonstrating the limitations of the government's inclusionary-corporatist project. Certainly, the CNA depended politically on the Velasco government, representing a state alternative to the independent peasant movement. However, it was far from being a mere instrument in the government's hands. While providing Velasco with general political support, it attempted to expand popular participation beyond the narrow limits of corporatist arrangements. It also questioned some economic policies damaging to the co-operative economy. Most importantly, it tried to tackle the notorious problem of agricultural prices by establishing producers' control of the marketing system. Remarkably, the CNA's activities in this area involved the first experience of co-operation with its political rival, the CCP, a co-operation which characterized the post-populist period.

CONCLUSION

By the end of the populist period, the cotton co-operative sector in Peru had run into social, economic, and political difficulties. Land reform conducted by the Velasco government led to a state-controlled co-operative movement. State controls on the co-operatives, combined with the preservation of the hacienda occupational hierarchy, generated internal social inequalities and bureaucratic management. State intervention also inhibited co-operativist attitudes among co-operative members which, in turn, affected their work performance and undermined the efficiency of co-operative agriculture.

At the same time, the co-operatives suffered the negative consequences of Velasco's economic strategies, which were adapted to the needs of ISI. The price controls policy considerably reduced co-operative profits, and these were further diminished by their having to pay the agrarian debt. In the case of cotton, co-operative profits were also adversely affected by the exchange rate and taxation policies discriminating against agricultural exporters. Moreover, by the end of Velasco's rule, the impact of all these policies was aggravated by the national economic crisis, which pushed up production costs while agricultural prices remained subject to state controls. The negative effect of these factors was, however, partly offset by the financial support offered by the Velasco government to the co-operative sector.

While the co-operative economy languished under the combined effect of the negative internal and external factors, the co-operative movement found itself in a political deadlock. It had developed under the direct control of the state, in confrontation with the independent peasant movement. This diminished the effectiveness of the political initiatives undertaken by the CNA in defence of the co-operative economy. The CNA's attempts to increase producers' participation in marketing agricultural products, which could have permitted producers to offset Velasco's price policies, ended in failure. While the CNA's efforts were viewed with increasing suspicion by the government, their futility was bound to disillusion its members.

The low economic and political viability of the post-reform co-operative movement facilitated a co-operative crisis in the late 1970s and early 1980s. The crisis itself, however, was precipitated by a change in government policies which marked the transition from the populist to the post-populist period.

CHAPTER THREE

Co-Operatives in the Post-Populist Context 1975-1983

The fall of Velasco marked the transition to the post-populist period characterized by a trend toward the liberalization of the national economy and the crisis of co-operative agriculture. The co-operatives fell out of favour with the government as the private sector came to be seen as the main agent of national agricultural development. Many co-operative members, tired of internal conflicts and government controls, welcomed this change in government economic policies. They advocated the dissolution of production co-operatives in the hope of obtaining access to individual plots of land. However, there was also considerable opposition within the co-operatives to the subdivision of land. Below, I discuss the development of the co-operative crisis after the fall of Velasco, as well as members' responses to this crisis.

AGRICULTURAL POLICIES AND CO-OPERATIVE ECONOMIC CRISIS

The demise of military populism in Peru was followed by a gradual shift of national economic strategies toward a free-market approach. This shift started under Morales, Velasco's successor. Upon the recommendations of the International Monetary Fund and private financial institutions, his administration implemented orthodox stabilization programs designed to improve the balance of payments and to curb inflation by exchange rate adjustments, fiscal restraint, and a general reduction of state economic activities.[1]

The shift to a free market economy continued during the civilian rule of Belaunde, who replaced Morales in 1980. Under Belaunde, economic neo-liberalism became a national economic philosophy. The new strategies were geared toward integrating the Peruvian economy more closely with the world economic system. They involved reliance on exports, which implied a continual devaluation of the Peruvian currency. They also implied further relaxation or total elimination of price controls, a continuation of cutbacks in government spending, and a more comprehensive program of privatization.[2]

The effects of the new economic strategies on the cotton co-operative economy could be expected to be mixed. Promoting exports and relaxing price controls could benefit cotton producers penalized under ISI arrangements, both as agricultural exporters and as suppliers of an industrial input. At the same time, the co-operative sector, created as a state-sponsored alternative to private capitalist agriculture, could be expected to lose the state support it had enjoyed during the military populist period. As will be shown, only the latter expectation proved to be correct. After a temporary recovery, Peruvian cotton production plummeted. In one year, from 1982 to 1983, the national output of cotton was halved. To an extent, the crisis reflected the downward trend in international cotton prices after 1980 (see Table 5).

The negative effect of this price trend, however, was reinforced and amplified by the post-populist economic policies. Despite a general commitment to relaxing state economic controls, Morales and, until 1983, Belaunde maintained the state monopoly of the cotton trade and Velasco's policy of low cotton prices. Over the second half of the 1970s, the floor prices of cotton in Peru (in 1970 *soles*) stagnated, even when the prices of Peruvian cotton in the international market kept rising (see Table 6). In other words, the post-populist price policies continued to benefit the textile interests at the expense of the cotton producers.[3]

Low cotton prices were aggravated by the growth in production costs which, after the fall of the Velasco government, became astronomical. Post-populist exchange policies were based on devaluation of the Peruvian currency, contrasting with the tight exchange controls practised by Velasco. Devaluation was designed to reduce national imports and to encourage export-related activities. In the case of cotton exports, however, its potentially stimulating effect was wiped out by the state-controlled prices. At the same time, the devaluation led to soaring costs for imported agricultural inputs (fuel, fertilizers, pesticides). It also pushed up consumer prices and agricultural wages. According to a study conducted by the Centre of Research for Development and Participation (CEDEP), cotton production costs increased seventeen times from 1973 to 1980, while cotton prices grew only nine times (see Table 7).

TABLE 5: International cotton prices (in US$) and Peruvian production of raw cotton (in T), 1975-83

	1975	1976	1977	1978	1979	1980	1981	1982	1983
Pima Cotton									
International prices	82	115	108	117	135	131	131	105	107
Tanguis cotton									
	64	101	92	86	99	103	99	75	84
Pima and Tanguis cotton									
Production	227	165	176	187	243	256	286	256	104

SOURCE: BCR, *Memoria* 1983:Tables 4 and 13

The situation in the food-crop sector seemed to be slightly better. Still, the growth of production costs for corn kept outpacing price increases during the entire period in question. The general trend for potatoes was the same, with the exception of some years. Only rice enjoyed relatively favourable terms of trade through most of the period.[4] Like cotton, rice marketing in Peru was controlled by the state. However, the price increases granted to rice farmers tended to be considerably higher than those obtained by cotton producers (see Table 7). This certainly made rice growing a potentially attractive alternative to cotton production. However, most cotton-growing valleys in Peru suffer from a shortage of water, and rice is irrigation-

TABLE 6: International and domestic Peruvian cotton prices, 1975-80

Average prices of Peruvian cotton in int'l mkt (per quintal of fibre)		Average floor prices to domestic producer (per kg of raw cotton)*	
	U.S.$	soles	1970 soles*
1975	71.9	18.799	10.376
1976	91.4	23.306	9.636
1977	103.3	35.584	10.659
1978	96.5	54.049	10.256
1979	113.7	99.946	11.309
1980	102.1	153.300	10.899

SOURCES: BCR *Memoria* 1982:Appendix 13; BCR *Reseña Económica 1982:62*; *Ministerio de Agricultura Estadística Agraria* December 1982:Table 24; Salaverry 1982:Table 1.6
*Calculated on the basis of consumer price indexes used as a substitute for agricultural deflators

TABLE 7: Evolving prices and costs of production for cotton, corn, potatoes, and rice, Peru, 1973-80 (1973 = 100)

	Cotton		Corn		Potatoes		Rice	
Years	Prices	Costs	Prices	Costs	Prices	Costs	Prices	Costs
1973	100	100	100	100	100	100	100	100
1974	109	117	126	104	123	79	120	142
1975	97	156	155	194	137	170	172	178
1976	120	194	161	—	153	196	175	212
1977	187	302	248	344	336	244	271	278
1978	278	498	455	590	415	409	460	380
1979	527	1,094	690	1,024	916	611	965	908
1980	866	1,704	1,057	1,659	1,660	1,796	1,290	1,284

SOURCE: Billone et al. 1982:Table 26

intensive. Potatoes seemed to be another possible alternative. However, they also required more water than cotton. In addition, after the liberalization of the potato market, potato prices had been extremely unstable, which diminished its attractiveness in areas with insufficient water resources. As a consequence, even when exposed to adverse trade terms, most cotton growers continued to rely on cotton as their major cash crop.

While the growing gap between the increase in production costs and cotton farm prices affected all cotton producers, its impact on profits seemed to be particularly disastrous for cotton co-operatives. This seemed to be partly due to declining individual work performance after land reform (see Chapter 2), which pushed up co-operative production costs in comparison with those of private producers. No less important, however, was the fact that after the Velasco government fell, the co-operative sector lost its privileged status over private agriculture. The first blow came with the introduction of a tax on co-operative profits which wiped out the tax exemptions the co-operative sector had enjoyed for more than a decade. The change in credit policy took longer, but its implications were even more devastating. Most post-reform agricultural co-operatives depended for their funding on the state-owned Agrarian Bank. During the Velasco administration, the Bank had functioned as a promotional agency, implementing low agricultural interest rates. Under Morales, the Bank continued this policy, maintaining its interest rates considerably below the national rates of inflation (see Table 8). As a consequence, it was not able to recover its funds without state financial assistance. Under the stabilization program, however, this assistance was becoming increasingly scarce, which forced the Bank to reduce its operations. In five years,

TABLE 8: Agrarian Bank interest rates on short-term agricultural loans and national rates of inflation, 1975-82

	1975	1976	1977	1978	1979	1980	1981	1982
Interest rates								
Co-operatives								
Food crops	7.0	10.0	14.0	14.0	—	—	—	—
Ind. crops	10.0	14.0	16.0	16.0	—	—	—	—
Private producers								
Small	7-10	10-14	16-17	16-17	—	—	—	—
Medium	7-12	10-14	16-17	16-17	—	—	—	—
Big	9-12	10-14	16-17	16-17	—	—	—	—
All producers								
Food crops	—	—	—	—	29.0	29.0	49.5	49.5
Ind. crops	—	—	—	—	32.0	32.0	49.5	49.5
Inflation rates	23.6	33.5	38.0	57.8	67.7	59.2	59.1	58.7

SOURCES: Salaverry 1982:Table 4.4; BCR *Memoria* 1982:Table 11; BCR *Reseña Económica* 1982:62

from 1975 to 1980, the amount of state agricultural credit, in 1970 *soles*, fell from 9 to 7 thousand million (Salaverry 1982:84).

This credit policy was reversed by Belaunde, who tried to put state agricultural credit on a commercial basis. In the 1980s, the Agrarian Bank expanded its funds, largely through foreign financing. At the same time, however, the Bank's interest rates were brought closer to the rates of inflation. Increasing the interest rates had a disastrous effect on agricultural co-operatives, many of which belonged to the category of high-cost producers, and were consequently much more sensitive to them than the low-cost private farmers. Moreover, in 1979, the co-operative sector was stripped of the preferential interest rates it had enjoyed during the Velasco and most of the Morales administrations. From that year on, the interest rates for co-operatives and private producers followed the same general guidelines (see Table 8). As for preferential rates, they were granted to private commercial initiatives, such as the development of the jungle areas undertaken mostly by transnational lumber corporations.[5]

The government's intention of using agricultural credit for encouraging private entreprise was made explicit by the 1980 Agrarian Promotion Law.[6] The Law confirmed the end of the co-operatives' privileged status with regard to state financial assistance. At the same time, it broadened the legal definition of agricultural activity, extending the eligibility for agricultural loans to companies involved in agricultural marketing and technical services. As a result of this modification, agricultural co-operatives had to compete for credit on equal terms, not only with private agricultural producers, but also with agribusiness. This considerably reduced their chances for obtaining loans. Moreover, state financial assistance itself became a trap, for the Agrarian Promotion Law permitted agricultural co-operatives to use their lands (non-negotiable since the 1969 land reform) as collateral for credit.

The post-populist agricultural policies, in effect, created an economic climate propitious for the disintegration of the post-reform co-operative sector. They were complemented by land policies which actually led to this disintegration. The expropriation and transfer of land under the 1969 land reform had been practically stopped by the end of Morales' rule. Belaunde's rise to power marked the beginning of a neo-liberal counter-reform. In the 1980s, the Land Court ordered a number of devolutions of expropriated land to their former owners (Matos Mar and Mejia 1980:175, Mejia 1980:31-3). The reasons for the devolutions varied. Most frequently, however, they were related to the co-operatives' abandonment of arable lands as a consequence of the co-operatives' financial crisis.

The Belaunde government also established a solid legal basis for dismantling the co-operative sector. The Agrarian Promotion Law authorized the Ministry of Agriculture to "restructure" co-operatives suffering from financial difficulties, internal conflicts, or smallholders' land invasions. According to the Law, the restructuring could involve the subdivision of co-operative lands into plots to be transferred to the ownership of both co-operative members and non-members, as well as the division of oversized co-operatives. These provisions served as a basis for the 1981 National Plan for the Reorganization of the Co-operative Sector, which included 154 agricultural production co-operatives and twenty-one highland livestock co-operatives. If fully implemented, the Plan would diminish the co-operative area considerably, transferring a large part of it to individual ownership. Under a free land market, this transfer would be accompanied by a massive sale of plots and probably lead eventually to the reconcentration of land into large private estates approximating the ownership pattern of pre-reform agriculture.[7]

Clearly, the post populist economic policies dealt a severe blow to co-operative agriculture in general and to cotton co-operatives in particular. The post-reform co-operatives lost state support for credit and taxation. In addition, however, and contrary to the general trend of economic liberalization, cotton prices through most of the period remained subject to state controls designed to benefit the domestic textile industry. While the post-populist governments shrank from liberalizing the cotton trade until 1983, most of their other economic policies closely followed the orthodox prescriptions. The devaluation of the Peruvian currency pushed up cotton production costs far beyond increases in cotton prices. The unfavourable terms of trade, combined with the elimination of credit and tax incentives for co-operative agriculture, drove cotton co-operatives to the brink of financial bankruptcy. The co-operative economic crisis was aggravated by the government land policies designed to privatize co-operative lands.

These agricultural and land policies could be expected to raise discontent among co-operative workers. The agricultural price and credit policies, whose effect on the co-operative cotton economy was particularly dramatic, were the most probable targets for co-operative opposition. The land policies, however, were likely to provoke a less negative response. While defending the co-operatives against outsiders, their members might still be interested in subdividing co-operative lands into plots, under the restructuring procedures established by the Agrarian Promotion Law. The long-standing internal organizational problems described in Chapter 2, as well as the more recent financial difficulties, would certainly spread such interest.

In effect, the ambiguity of co-operative workers' attitudes about the post-populist economic policies manifested itself in two contradictory trends within the national co-operative movement. While the national co-operative leadership succeeded in organizing a nation-wide political mobilization against government economic policies, many individual co-operatives started subdividing, succumbing to the post-populist pressure for economic liberalization.

CO-OPERATIVE POLITICAL MOBILIZATION

The shift toward economic orthodoxy in Peru was accompanied by a considerable deterioration in the standards of living of the popular sectors. The stabilization programs conducted by the military government of Morales led to a dramatic decline in real wages. Although the wage restraints were somewhat relaxed after the return to civilian rule in 1980, real wages remained low because of the high rates of inflation (see Table 9).

The decline in real wages affected both urban workers and agricultural labourers, including members of the agricultural production co-operatives who depended on wages for their major source of income. In addition, the recession led to a growth in unemployment. This growth skyrocketed after Morales suppressed the Labour Stability Law passed under Velasco. In agricultural production co-operatives,

TABLE 9: Real average and minimum wages in metropolitan Lima, in *soles* per month, 1975-82

	1975	1976	1977	1978	1979	1980	1981*	1982*
Av. wages	4,658	5,020	3,987	3,535	3,639	4,059	3,651	3,837
Min. wages	2,295	2,102	1,817	1,337	1,743	2,111	1,023	1,589

SOURCES: Dietz 1982:84; *Proceso Económico*, 1 Oct. 1982
*Average wages in February in the private sector; minimum wages in June

labour stability for members was still guaranteed by co-operative statutes. However, the rapid increase in production costs raised the problem of redundancy in this sector of the national economy as well, creating inside pressure for the co-operatives to reduce their labour force.

The decline in real wages and the problem of unemployment after the fall of the Velasco government spread social and political unrest.[8] In an attempt to demobilize labour unions and participatory organizations created during the Velasco period (agricultural co-operatives included), Morales declared a state of emergency, prohibiting all organizational political activities. The political repression under the state of emergency far exceeded the repression used by Velasco at the end of his rule and sharply contrasted with his earlier inclusionary-corporatist policies. It indicated that government participatory strategies had shifted from the political incorporation of the popular sectors to their political exclusion.

In the co-operative movement, the exclusionary strategies involved increased state administrative and political controls. In 1976, the controls on co-operative wages were tightened to the point of practically eliminating the co-operatives' already limited autonomy in this area. At the same time, the scope of operation of SAF-CAP (System for Assisting and Auditing Agricultural Production Co-operatives), a state agency engaged in supervising sugar co-operatives, was expanded. Under the new regulations, SAF-CAP was authorized to intervene in all types of agricultural co-operatives, with the objective of auditing their finances, appointing the managerial staff, and controlling wages. Moreover, in response to growing discontent among sugar co-operative workers, SAF-CAP was also authorized to disqualify co-operative members involved in organizing co-operative strikes (García-Sayán 1977:147-8). In 1977, the government intervened in eleven agricultural co-operatives in Alto Piura. The intervention was followed by freezing co-operative wages, reducing the co-operatives' staffs, and eventually by transferring most of the co-operative lands to the individual ownership of co-operative members and local smallholders.

While increasing state control of the post-reform co-operative movement, Morales also purged those pro-Velasco officers and their civilian advisers who had provided it with political and institutional support. This measure had unexpectedly far-reaching political implications. In a spectacular break with their previous inclusionary-corporatist position, some purged officers organized the Socialist Revolutionary Party (PSR), under the leadership of the former director of SINAMOS, General (r) Leonidas Rodriguez Figueroa. The main base of the new party's popular support was the CNA, representing the post-reform co-operative movement. Under PSR leadership, the CNA rapidly mounted political opposition to Morales. Along with the independent labour and peasant federations, the CNA participated in the 1978 national general strike.[9] Furthermore, it took a critical stance toward the elections for the National Constituent Assembly, which marked the beginning of the transition to civilian rule. The CNA criticized the Assembly electoral regulations which excluded illiterates (peasants or agricultural labourers for the most part) from the electoral process and claimed the right to participate in the elections as a functional organization representing agricultural interests (CNA 1977c). The CNA's claim was rejected by the Electoral Jury, which, however, did not prevent its leaders from running under the PSR banner.

The CNA's political activism demonstrated the failure of the government's attempts to increase control of the co-operative movement and eventually forced it to modify its exclusionary strategies. In 1978, on the eve of elections for the National Constituent Assembly, Morales issued a decree dismantling CNA and, consequently, excluding it legally from the national institutional arena. This measure was justified by reference to the CNA's politicization. It had, however, more profound causes related to the structural changes which had been taking place since the demise of military populism. The CNA represented co-operative agriculture which, in the post-populist context, was relegated to the very margin of government concerns. The protagonist of agricultural development became once again the agrarian bourgeoisie which, since the dissolution of the National Agricultural Society (SNA), had had no institutional access to national politics. At the regional level, however, it was still represented by a number of agricultural associations. In addition, in many cases, the bourgeoisie had gained control of the local and regional Committees of Agricultural Producers organized by the CNA.

The revival of the politically notorious SNA did not appeal to Morales, even though it had been requested by some regional agricultural associations. Instead, he opted for detaching the Committees of Agricultural Producers from the CNA and reaffiliating them with a new national body, the National Agrarian Organization (ONA). In 1978, the ONA replaced the CNA as the official representative of agrarian interests. It was granted representation in government agencies, such as the Agrarian Bank and ENCI, previously the privilege of the CNA. It also took over the CNA's sources of financing, including state subsidies and the 0.5 per cent tax on co-operative sales.

Ironically, the end of the CNA's official existence coincided with the beginning of the transition to civilian rule, closing the period of political exclusion of the popular organizations.[10] The return to liberal democracy offered the CNA new opportunities for political action. It could be expected to use these opportunities for exerting political pressure in defence of the co-operative sector threatened by the post-populist agricultural price and credit policies as well as the prospect of the neo-liberal counter-reform. However, the ambivalent position of co-operative members on the subdivision of co-operative land made the counter-reform an unsuitable rallying point for co-operative political mobilization. Moreover, the effectiveness of this mobilization depended, to a large extent, on the CNA's ability to gain political support from other agrarian organizations, such as the CCP and the ONA. Both organizations represented, respectively, the poor peasants and the agrarian bourgeoisie, each with a stake in land redistribution. Realizing the controversial implications of the post-populist land policies, the CNA leadership opted for a co-operative mobilization against price and credit policies, which it hoped to use as the basis for forging a broad agrarian opposition.[11]

In the early 1980s, the prospects for a joint agrarian opposition looked relatively bright. The two other major agrarian organizations, the CCP and the ONA, shared the CNA's concern with price and credit policies. For the CCP, this was a relatively new preoccupation. As already mentioned, after land reform, the CCP became the main representative of peasants excluded from land redistribution and interested mostly in increasing their access to it. The land question clearly dominated the agenda at the CCP's Fifth Congress in 1978. At the 1982 Congress, however, the top priority shifted to the question of government agricultural policies.[12] This question was raised most forcefully by the delegates from the Departmental Agrarian Federation of Piura and Tumbes (FRADEPT), which represented Piura cotton-growing co-operatives and peasant communities severely affected by the economic crisis. Their demands were practically identical with those of cotton co-operatives channelled by the CNA. Moreover, the delegates also called for co-operation with the CNA in defence of the co-operative economy.[13] The demands of the cotton producers were supported by the CCP national leadership, whose attitude toward the rival CNA had improved considerably after the CNA had broken its ties with the government and moved into political opposition.

Although the CCP had only recently shown interest in agricultural price and credit policies, the ONA had always been interested in them on behalf of the small and medium capitalist producers it represented. In the 1980s, the ONA exerted considerable political pressure to moderate the impact of economic neo-liberalism on small and medium private agriculture. Its opposition to the government's policies was particularly noticeable in the cotton trade, the liberalization of which raised loud protests from the Cotton Committee, one of the ONA's Committees of Agricultural Producers.

The cross-organizational convergence of cotton interests manifested itself in a twenty-four-hour cotton strike in August 1982. The strike was called by the national Cotton Committee and supported by both the CNA and the CCP. The strikers demanded higher cotton prices, the preservation of the state monopoly in the cotton trade, and better credit facilities. The government's reluctance to meet these demands induced the CNA to try to step up the political pressure, extending the strike to other agricultural sectors. In November 1982, it called for a forty-eight-hour national agrarian strike, demanding higher prices for cotton, sugar, corn, wheat, and other crops, as well as an increase in Agrarian Bank funds and lower interest rates. In addition, it included more general demands, such as the abolition of the Agrarian Promotion Law.[14] The strike platform was signed by the CNA, the CCP, and some other minor agrarian organizations, but not by the Cotton Committee and the ONA, whose national leadership was obviously uncomfortable with the political thrust of the strikers' demands.

The ONA's unwillingness to support the national agrarian strike raised questions about the viability of the CNA's strategy of joint agrarian opposition. In the case of the ONA, the problem had a clearly political character. Within the post-populist framework, the ONA represented the interests of the small and medium agrarian bourgeoisie who expected to benefit from the disintegration of the co-operative sector, as well as from the government's incentives for private agriculture. Certainly, the ONA was trying to increase its influence through political alliances in order to protect its membership from the adverse effects of both state controls and economic neo-liberalism. Accordingly, it was willing to co-operate with the CNA on limited issues such as agricultural marketing, prices, and credit. However, even this limited co-operation remained half-hearted. The ONA's membership had already obtained special privileges no longer available to the co-operative sector: representation in government agencies, new lines of credit for private producers, and subsidies for technical assistance.

While the ONA proved to be a rather unreliable ally, the alliance between the CNA and the CCP proved no less problematic. Even though the CCP endorsed the national agrarian strike (in contrast to the Cotton Committee and the ONA in general), its actual involvement was not very impressive. The only notable exception was the sugar co-operative sector, where the CCP had increased its presence since the economic crisis began. The limited participation of the CCP membership in the CNA-initiated strike could be partly explained by the persistence of political and ideological differences which both organizations had inherited from military populism. These differences were particularly acute at the leadership level. More important than the CCP leaders' political reservations about the strike, however, was its limited ability to mobilize most of its membership against agricultural policies.

As already mentioned, the main source of the CCP's organizational strength after land reform was the highland community peasants. As the events of the 1970s demonstrated, they could be relatively easily mobilized against land invasions, but not so readily against price and credit policies. To begin with, most community peasants had been excluded from land reform and had limited access to land. Accordingly, the land question in the highlands overshadowed the problems of marketing, prices, and credit, which were crucial for the coastal agricultural co-operatives formed from expropriated haciendas. Furthermore, in the peasant sector the problems of prices and credit had no direct relation to agricultural policies. While the co-operative sector's marketing and credit were controlled by the state, the peasants sold most of their produce to private traders and relied for financial assistance on private moneylenders. As a consequence, the demands for higher (state-controlled) prices and better (state-controlled) credit facilities were irrelevant to them. Finally, the very nature of the peasant economy was not conducive to organized political action against price and credit policies. The production co-operatives relied almost exclusively on large-scale commercial agriculture. This made them extremely vulnerable to changes in the national economic conjuncture and, at the same time, unable or unwilling to escape the logic of market relations. In contrast, the highland peasants could fall back on production for family consumption (rearranging and minimizing their ties with the market) when confronted with an unfavourable market conjuncture.

The combined effect of these and other factors accounted for the relatively low level of community peasant participation in the national agrarian strike. This low level of participation, along with the practical non-participation of small and medium capitalist producers, reduced the strike's political effectiveness and raised serious doubts about the viability of rural political alliances.

In sum, the transition from military populism to post-populism in Peru changed the political nature of the post-reform co-operative movement, as represented by the CNA. Stabilization programs were accompanied by the government's attempts to exclude it politically, which led to a breakdown of the previous inclusionary-corporatist arrangements. After the return to liberal democracy, the CNA reappeared in the national arena as an independent political actor, concentrating on agricultural price and credit policies. In part, this choice was dictated by the desperate economic situation of the co-operative sector. However, it also reflected the fact that, in contrast to the land tenure counter-reform, price and credit policies had an adverse effect upon a wide range of agricultural producers, thereby providing a potential basis for co-operation among various agrarian organizations.

The CNA leadership, however, seemed to overrate the unifying effect of post-populist agricultural policies. While objecting to the low state-controlled agricultural prices, the liberalization of agricultural trade, and high interest rates, the small and medium agrarian bourgeoisie represented by the ONA expected to benefit from the government's incentives for private agriculture, as well as from the policy of land tenure counter-reform. Conversely, the CCP's efforts to mobilize highland peasants were not very successful. This was partly due to the peasants' demands for land remaining largely unsatisfied. In addition, the organization of peasant agriculture as such, with its persistent reliance on production for family consumption and its dependence on private traders and moneylenders, made peasant mobilization against price and credit policies extremely problematic.

The difficulties involved in organizing a joint agrarian opposition diminished the CNA's capacity to use the new political space opened after the transition to liberal democracy in defence of the co-operative agricultural sector. These difficulties also raised questions about the longer term political behaviour of its own membership — the co-operative labour force. Confronted with the economic crisis, would most co-operative members defend the co-operative sector, responding to the CNA's call for political mobilization? Or, following the example of small capitalist producers, would they welcome the division of co-operative lands and the resurgence of private agriculture? The answers to these questions are not self-apparent. The unprecedented co-operative political mobilization of the early 1980s was paralleled by a movement for the subdivision of co-operative lands, leading to a virtual disintegration of the post-reform co-operative sector.

SUBDIVISION OF CO-OPERATIVE LANDS: WORKERS AGAINST CO-OPERATIVES?

The political mobilization against agricultural policies was one outcome of the co-operative economic crisis which developed in the late 1970s and early 1980s. The other was the subdivision of co-operative lands, resulting in the partial disintegration of the post-reform co-operative sector.[15] Reflecting the co-operative workers' discontent with the poor condition of the co-operative economy, subdivison appeared as an individualistic, non-political alternative to co-operative mobilization. The relative attractiveness of this alternative for the workers could be explained by the persistence of organizational problems within the post-reform co-operative movement discussed in Chapter 2. The relation between these problems and the subdivision of co-operative lands was emphasized by Petras and Havens (1981). According to them, the bureaucratization of the co-operative movement created a basis for the emergence of anti-co-operative attitudes among the hacienda workers (peasants in Petras' and Havens' terminology), despite the fact that they had been the major beneficiaries of land reform: "The peasants linked central bureaucratic control with local [intra-co-operative] exploitation and perceived both as irrational mechanisms for maximizing production and minimizing local [co-operative] collective and individual benefits" (Petras and Havens 1981:235).

Given this anti-co-operative orientation among the hacienda workers, the deterioration in their situation led to a movement for the subdivision of co-operative lands rather than to a defence of the co-operative economy. Viewed in this perspective, the movement was directed primarily against state-controlled forms of co-operativism. As such, it was congenial to the anti-co-operative peasant movement encouraged by the CCP in the 1970s (Petras and Havens 1981:230-3).

The argument advanced by Petras and Havens, no matter how convincing, ignores the opposite trend in the co-operative movement in the early 1980s, that is, the political mobilization discussed earlier in this chapter. It seems that at least some sectors of the co-operative labour force had developed a relatively strong co-operative commitment and provided organizational support for the CNA-led mobilization against agricultural policies. What factors accounted for this political ambivalence of the co-operative membership in the face of the economic crisis?

Possible answers can be found in Méndez's study of subdivison in coastal agricultural co-operatives (Méndez 1982). Rather than explaining the subdivision in terms of the state-sponsored origins of the post-reform co-operative movement, Méndez relates it primarily to the co-operative financial crisis which, to a large extent, reflected changes in agricultural prices, interest rates, and production costs as discussed earlier. While emphasizing the role of government economic policies in the decline of the co-operative economy, she also points out that the exorbitant growth of co-operative production costs was partly caused by the co-operative members' attempts to obtain immediate individual and collective benefits at the expense of the co-operative economy as a whole. Among these, she mentions the pressure for higher wages and better social services as well as relaxed labour discipline and the increasing reliance on temporary and quasi-temporary labour. From this perspective, the subdivision of co-operative lands appears to increase the efficiency of the co-operative economy by transforming the single production units into service co-operatives composed of individual producers. According to the advocates of subdivision, this transformation would induce the membership of the new service co-operatives to improve their work performance, to reduce the use of temporary and quasi-temporary labour, and to incorporate unpaid family labour into productive activities.

Méndez's interviews with co-operative workers indicate that many expressed these views in one form or another. Many other respondents, however, rejected subdivision, arguing that it would deprive the workers of the economic benefits offered by production co-operatives and that it would eventually lead to the sale of individual holdings. The prospect of losing the relative economic security inherent in the production co-operatives was certainly a powerful deterrent against subdivision. This deterrent could be expected to be particularly effective for co-operative field workers whose limited economic resources hardly left them able to become successful commercial farmers after subdivision. However, if Petras and Havens are to be believed, it was precisely these workers who sought to rid themselves of the bureaucratic, exploitative production co-operatives. How can these apparently contradictory sets of arguments be reconciled? And what was the role of relatively well-off members of the co-operative bureaucracy with respect to subdivision? They certainly had vested interests in the co-operative system but, at the same time, they also had a reasonable chance for economic success as private farmers. Consequently, they might have been even more interested in the subdivision of co-operative lands than were the field workers. If this were true, the movement for subdivision would acquire a rather peculiar character.

Instead of being a manifestation of worker and peasant opposition to the state-controlled co-operativism, as Petras and Havens suggest, it would be part of the post-populist ascendance of the agrarian bourgeoisie, emerging, in this case, from inside the co-operative movement.

CONCLUSION

The transition to post-populism in Peru has profoundly changed the post-reform co-operative movement. This change, facilitated by the breakdown of the inclusionary-corporatist institutions, took place in response to the co-operative economic crisis. This was triggered by the agricultural and land policies pursued by the Morales and the Belaunde governments as part of a general shift toward economic neo-liberalism. In the cotton sector, the co-operative crisis was caused primarily by the continuation of Velasco's policy of cotton price controls, coupled with the introduction of neo-liberal credit policies which boosted co-operative expenses. The economic crisis was aggravated by the prospect of the privatization of co-operative lands which was encouraged by Belaunde's counter-reform policies.

The critical situation in which the co-operative sector found itself after the Velasco government fell evoked two responses among the co-operative membership. One was a political mobilization against agricultural price and credit policies. This response was promoted by the CNA which, since the fall of Velasco, had gained political autonomy and had adopted a strategy of joint agrarian opposition. The other response was a subdivision of co-operative lands which amounted to a tacit acceptance of the government's pressure for counter-reform. What factors accounted for this acceptance and how profound was it?

One line of analysis followed by Petras and Havens focuses on the distorted, state-controlled character of the post-reform co-operative movement. Viewed from this perspective, the economic crisis served as a catalyst for the growing discontent with this movement among the co-operative workers. Accordingly, they could be expected to reject both the state-controlled forms of co-operation and the CNA-led mobilization, opting instead for the subdivision of co-operative lands. The other approach, as advanced by Méndez, is less deterministic about the outcomes of the co-operative crisis. It focuses on the immediate causes of the crisis, rather than on the structural origins of the co-operative movement. More specifically, it emphasizes the workers' more or less successful attempts to maximize their immediate economic gains in disregard of the long-term success of the co-operative economy imposed on them by the state. In this approach, the co-operative workers appear to be ambivalent toward subdivision. While attracted by family agriculture, they are also reluctant to lose the economic benefits offered to them by production co-operatives. As a consequence, they may support both the movement for subdivision and the CNA-led mobilization, depending on circumstances.

Which line of analysis is more appropriate for understanding the outcomes of the co-operative crisis is determined in Part Two, using case studies of three cotton production co-operatives organized after land reform began.

PART TWO: THE COTTON CO-OPERATIVES:
A HISTORY OF SUCCESS AND FAILURE

CHAPTER FOUR

The Origin and Socio-Economic Organization of the Cotton Co-Operatives

By the time of land reform, agriculture in the valley selected for the case studies had reached a relatively high level of capitalist development. During the 1950s and 1960s, it underwent rapid modernization involving an expansion of irrigated areas and a consolidation of centrally managed cotton haciendas. Local haciendas had been involved in cotton growing throughout the century. However, during the first half of the century, most hacienda owners relied on sharecropping, leasing all or large parts of their lands to small tenants, *yanaconas*, mostly in exchange for rent in kind or labour. An increase in international cotton prices during the interwar period spurred local cotton production. Some of the most successful growers started to invest in drilling irrigation wells, trying to tap subterranean water resources abundant in the valley. These resources permitted them to expand and stabilize irrigation, which boosted cotton productivity.

The trend toward capitalist modernization accelerated in the late 1940s and in the 1950s. After a sharp decline during the Second World War, the international demand for cotton started to rise again. Domestic consumption also grew, boosted by the development of the national textile industry. Increased demand stimulated a further expansion of irrigated areas. During the 1950s and 1960s, Anderson Clayton, a principal cotton export company in Peru controlled by U.S. capital, carried out minor irrigation projects in the valley — drilling wells, installing water pumps, and building canals at the request of local cotton growers. They were assisted in their modernizing by the state-owned Agrarian Bank, which provided generous credits. The irrigation infrastructure was also improved by the construction of a dam in the mountains which regulated the flow of the local river.

By the time of the land reform, though, the development of irrigated areas in the valley had come to a halt, and a reverse process had started. Because of the uncontrolled use of subterranean waters, irrigation wells had begun to dry up. Some were replaced by new, deeper ones; nevertheless, since the end of the 1960s irrigation capacity had generally dropped.[1]

Irrigation agriculture increased the use of wage labour and contributed to the gradual disintegration of the system of *yanaconaje* (see Chapter 2). Some *yanaconas* obtained property titles; others were evicted by their landlords and subsequently became wage labourers on the centrally managed cotton haciendas. Still others continued to rent land from hacienda owners, but were gradually transformed into cash tenants. Thus, while some local haciendas completed the transition to direct production, others continued to rely on rental arrangements. I will refer to the former haciendas as centrally managed or centralized, and to the latter as decentralized.

The centrally managed cotton haciendas developed into relatively complex capitalist entreprises and became involved in large-scale mechanized irrigation agriculture. Their stable labour force had three easily identifiable occupational groups: the technical-administrative staff also known as employees (a manager, office clerks, overseers), the skilled workers (such as tractor drivers, mechanics, well operators) and the field workers or labourers. Although the first two groups clearly fell into the category of wage earners, the position of the field labourers was more ambiguous. Some owned or rented plots (less than 6 ha) which provided them with additional income. Accordingly, in most cases, the field labourers worked in the hacienda by "task," roughly five hours per day (from 7 a.m. to 12 noon), while the employees and the skilled workers had an 8-hour working day. This schedule left the field labourers with a free afternoon to devote to work on their plots or other jobs (such as breeding animals, working as farm hands or taking care of family business).

Apart from the stable field labourers, cotton haciendas employed many quasi-temporary labourers (temporary labourers employed on a more or less permanent basis). They were hired and fired every two or three months and worked without contracts for wages considerably lower than those earned by the stable field labourers. On some haciendas the quasi-temporary labourers performed most of agricultural operations, while the stable labourers were put in charge of semi-skilled jobs, such as irrigation or night watch. For the most part, these quasi-temporary labourers were either relatives (primarily adult children and wives) of the stable hacienda labourers or recent migrants from the highlands (Sierra), attracted by the agricultural expansion in the valley. In addition, cotton haciendas hired a large number of cotton pickers during the harvest. They were recruited mostly among seasonal migrants from the Sierra, but also, to a lesser extent, among local smallholders. The quasi-temporary (but not the stable) labourers participated in the harvest as well. The decentralized cotton haciendas had a similar internal structure which, however, was complicated by a vast sector of small tenants who could also hire their own temporary labourers and/or work on the haciendas for wages.

The managerial centralization of cotton estates was followed by the unionization of their labour forces. This process, however, developed mostly among stable field labourers. The seasonal cotton pickers and the quasi-temporary labourers were excluded. This adversely affected both their economic position and their organizational experiences. As for the unionized stable labourers, they succeeded in obtaining multiple concessions from the hacienda owners, such as shorter working days, social and health insurance, and better housing.

The first hacienda unions in the valley were organized by the politically moderate American Popular Revolutionary Alliance (APRA), a populist party extensively involved in rural unionism. The unions became affiliated with the National Federation of Peruvian Peasants (FENCAP) controlled by APRA. Shortly before land reform, however, many unions had radicalized their demands and changed their affiliation to the General Confederation of Peruvian Workers (CGTP) controlled by the Peruvian Communist Party. Rural mobilization peaked after the promulgation of the 1969 land reform. Many hacienda unions played an important role in curbing the resistance of local landlords and in accelerating the expropriation and adjudication of haciendas.

As elsewhere in Peru, land reform in the valley was controlled by the regional branches of the Ministry of Agriculture and SINAMOS. The reform affected not only haciendas exceeding the legal limit, but also a large number of smaller estates — if their owners practised indirect forms of cultivation (tenancy) or if they were accused by workers of violating labour legislation. By 1980, the Ministry of Agriculture had expropriated 182 estates with an aggregate cultivated area of 14,000 ha, that is, more than one-third of the total cultivated area in the valley. Convinced of the advantages of large-scale agriculture and pressed by the scarcity of irrigated land, land reform officials opted for large production co-operatives.[2] As a result, the 182 estates were transformed into twenty agricultural production co-operatives; only two service co-operatives based on small-scale individual production were created. Membership in the production co-operatives was granted to all stable workers and employees willing to join. It was also extended to many quasi-temporary labourers and tenants on the condition that the latter hand over their plots to the co-operative. Thus, the co-operative communities included extremely heterogeneous groups — a source of future internal tensions and conflicts.

I will now analyse the pre-reform and co-operative organization at Alamos, Siglo XX, and Monte Blanco.

ALAMOS: FROM A CENTRALLY MANAGED HACIENDA TO AN INDEPENDENT CO-OPERATIVE

Hacienda Alamos was formed in 1953 after Anderson Clayton completed irrigation work in a previously uncultivated area. In addition to cotton exports and irrigation projects, the company also grew cotton. Alamos became one of its first landed properties in the valley. It was a small, but highly centralized hacienda: practically all of its 400 ha of irrigated land were used for direct cultivation. The stable labour force at Alamos included seven employees, eight skilled workers and thirty-six field labourers. In addition to these, the hacienda management employed between ten and fifteen quasi-temporary labourers and approximately 100 cotton pickers (see Table 10).

The way in which the hacienda was formed strongly influenced its labour force. Virtually all the stable workers at Alamos were recruited the same year from a nearby settlement which consisted of a relatively small number of families, mostly of local origin. This settlement had its own elementary school; consequently, almost all the hacienda workers were literate. In 1962, the workers formed a hacienda union. They were assisted by APRA which, from that moment on, succeeded in maintaining it under APRA influence. The union had a relatively peaceful history. It dedicated itself to "pragmatic" negotiations with the hacienda management, gaining wage increases, labour stability, and social insurance benefits for its members.

The hacienda routine was broken on the eve of land reform, when the company decided to sell the hacienda, partly because its expropriation seemed inevitable and partly because the irrigation wells were drying up (by the late 1960s, one-fourth of the previously irrigated lands had been abandoned because of the shortage of water). The union insisted that the hacienda should be sold "along with its personnel," that is, that the new owners should take it over with all its workers. The prospective buyers, however, were reluctant to do so, probably intending to replace the organized, relatively well-paid

TABLE 10: Occupational structure at Alamos, Siglo XX, and Monte Blanco before and after co-operativization

	Alamos		Siglo XX		Monte Blanco	
	Hacienda 1969	Co-operative 1981	Hacienda 1972	Co-operative 1981	Hacienda 1973*	Co-operative 1981
Employees	7	1	18	41	6	16
Skilled Workers	8	8	20	116	9	22
Stable field workers	36	50	260	257	38	58
Total stable labour force	51	59	298	414	53	96

SOURCE: Co-operative accounts and interviews
*Decentralized area not included

workers with cheap, unorganized labour. When the union's request could not be satisfied, the workers decided to buy the hacienda and transform it into a production co-operative. This was done in 1969. According to the sales contract, the total cost of the hacienda (including 300 ha of irrigated and 700 ha of unirrigated lands, four wells with oil pumps, and four tractors) was 3 million *soles*. The down payment was made with the company's worker compensation funds which otherwise would have been paid to individual workers. The rest was to be paid out of co-operative profits over a ten-year period. The sale was ratified by the Ministry of Agriculture. The land reform officials, however, accepted the new co-operative without much enthusiasm: it was considered a case of "private reform" outside of the mainstream co-operative movement.

The co-operativization of hacienda Alamos was accompanied by a radical change in its socio-economic organization. Five of seven hacienda employees, including the engineer-agronomist (the manager), the overseers, and most of the office clerks left as soon as it was purchased by the worker union. One of the two remaining employees, the assistant agronomist who had played a vital role in the co-operativization of the hacienda, was unanimously elected as the new co-operative manager. He and the other employee, a bookkeeper, were allowed to retain their employee status and their relatively high salaries. The other jobs previously performed by employees were assigned to workers who continued to receive regular workers' wages. Most appointments were made through general elections. The overseer (now called the field supervisor) and the warehousekeeper were elected annually by the General Assembly. The functions of cashier and payroll clerk were performed by two members of the Administrative Council, also elected annually. The main reason for elections was to avoid corruption among those who, due to their job, had permanent access to the co-operative's funds. According to all interviewed workers, the new system proved to be very effective. "We are still making it here [despite the crisis] and other co-operatives have already broken down. That's because of mismanagement. The *criollo* people are very smart, you know. If they can snatch something, they'll do it. Here, it's different. Every year, we change all of them: the councils, the field supervisor, the cashier, the warehouse keeper. And the warehouse keeper is such a delicate position! Just imagine how much money goes through his hands!" (field labourer)

Only two office jobs, those of field technician and bookkeeper (the former bookkeeper became the manager after the death of the first co-operative manager), were permanently assigned to two young workers, though they continued to be paid the same wages as before their promotion. As a consequence of these changes, the employee category practically disappeared at Alamos (see Table 10).

The Alamos workers went even further in their reformist zeal. In 1971, the General Assembly decided to equalize co-operative incomes, raising field labourers' wages to those of skilled workers. The skilled workers also lost a significant portion of their supplementary payments (e.g., for night work), to which they were entitled under the existing labour legislation. Under the new regulations, the tractor drivers (frequently in the field from ten to twelve hours a day) were allowed to receive only two hours of overtime. The well operators (who stayed on duty twenty-four hours every other day) received the same overtime.

The new arrangement was bitterly resented by some skilled workers who felt that their work was no longer properly rewarded.

"First we tried to argue. It's not the same, we said, working with a spade that costs seven thousand [soles] and a tractor that costs twenty million. But they [the field labourers] don't understand. They just laugh at us: if you don't like to drive a tractor, take a spade. And we wanted to do it, as they did in S.D. [a neighbouring co-operative]. There, tractor drivers rebelled, left their tractors and went to work in the field like everybody else. So, the co-operative had to pay them extra. But here we didn't do it. After thirty years on a tractor, it's a bit difficult, you know, to go and work with a spade . . . but you'll see, it will be different with the younger ones, those who come to replace us. They would not want to toil for nothing as we do. My son, for example, doesn't want to learn driving a tractor. And he is right. What for? It's better to get fat working with a spade." (well operator)

This discontent, however, did not develop into an open conflict, largely due to strong internal social solidarity. For instance, this solidarity prevented well operators from following the advice of a visiting engineer and filing a complaint against the co-operative administration with Labour Inspection. "How could we do it? If we are all friends here, if we have known each other for God knows how long!" exclaimed one interviewed well operator. A more elaborate explanation was offered by another well operator who had been a co operative leader for a long time:

"That's what we decided from the very beginning. We are all peasants and we all have to earn the same. Why should I earn more if I know how to look after pumps? . . . It's not hard, everybody can learn it. I myself learned it here, in the hacienda. And I don't agree that the skilled workers should have higher wages. That's how all inequalities start. First come the skilled workers and then the employees, in neckties, sitting all day in the office. In other co-operatives, I've seen with my own eyes, whole trucks are coming loaded with Coke. Have you ever seen a peasant drinking Coke?" (well operator) [Symptomatically, Alamos was the only one of the three co-operatives that had no stall with soft drinks and cigarettes.]

As a consequence of the co-operative wage policies, there was practically no pressure for internal promotions. Not only did the group of employees disappear as such, but there was no change in the number of skilled labourers in the co-operative (see Table 10). The relative homogeneity of the co-operative occupational and income structure prevented deep intraco-operative antagonisms and relieved the field labourers' pressure for higher wages. In comparison with the two other co-operatives, wages in Alamos were relatively low. The dividends distributed among members at the end of the year were not impressive either: the workers continued to depend on wages for their living (see Table 11).

Like most other co-operatives, Alamos provided its members with some additional monetary and non-monetary benefits. The co-operative, for instance, distributed part of its food crops free to members. It also sold them some staples at low prices and granted them interest-free personal loans. I must emphasize, however, that co-operative services were kept to a minimum. Neither after co-operativization nor in 1979, when the co-operative made good profits because of the cotton price increase, did it launch ambitious social programs so typical of the other two co-operatives.

While wages and social services at Alamos remained modest, the working day was relatively long. In 1971, the wage equalization was complemented by introducing an eight-hour working day for field labourers. This decision might be viewed (as indeed it was by the resentful skilled workers) as merely a justification for increasing their wages. However, it also reflected a genuine concern with the outcome of the co-operative venture: "We used to work really hard those first years. We worked on Sundays, we permitted ourselves no wage increases, no bonuses. That's because we were afraid to fail. We were afraid that the cooperative wouldn't bring profits" (tractor driver). Recently, however, the field labourers' enthusiasm seems to have diminished. In 1980, a shorter working day was established for the summer. There were also indications of some relaxing of labour discipline. This was attributed by many informants to the excessive permissiveness of the new manager. However, the main reason seemed to be a trend toward the stagnation and even deterioration of the members' real incomes. In the late 1970s and early 1980s, the co-

TABLE 11: Real monthly wages of field workers and annual dividends at Alamos, Siglo XX, and Monte Blanco, 1975-81 (per 1,000 *soles* in 1985 currency)

	1975	1976	1977	1978	1979	1980	1981
Alamos							
Wages*	3,360	3,730	3,350	2,773	2,412	3,090	3,350
Dividends	3,050	6,661	2,184	2,615	11,099	4,820	0
Siglo XX							
Wages**	3,150	3,437	3,288	3,575	3,350	5,435	3,819
Dividends	6,900	5,340	6,552	9,688	6,270	0	0
Monte Blanco							
Wages**	2,700	3,197	3,105	3,405	3,068	—	3,264
Dividends	8,648	6,566	4,723	6,247	10,368	0	0

SOURCE: Co-operative accounts
* 8-hour working day
** 5-hour working day

operative wage increases were wiped out by mounting rates of inflation. The decline in real incomes caused co-operative members to turn
to private economic activities and, consequently, to seek a shorter
working day in the co-operative:

"We've always worked here eight hours a day, that's why we are better off than
most other co-operatives. Only this year we decided to change it, to work from
six to twelve, five hours, but to work with conscientiousness . . . It's better like
this. And in the afternoon one has time to do other things: if one has a farm, to
work on the farm; if one has animals, to look after the animals. The problem is
that prices go up every day. What we earn here is not enough any more." (field
labourer)

Nevertheless, complementary private activities at Alamos remained
remarkably modest as compared to the situation in the other two co-
operatives.

SIGLO XX: STATE-SPONSORED CO-OPERATIVE ON A CENTRALLY MANAGED ESTATE

Hacienda Siglo XX was established at the turn of the century by an
Italian immigrant who started by selling scissors and who ended up as
one of the wealthiest men in Peru. Upon his arrival in the valley he
married a woman from a local Indian community which owned a
considerable part of the valley at that time. This gave him the right of
land ownership within the community boundaries. In addition to
agriculture and retail trade, he became involved in usury, investing his
profits in land inside and outside the community, and later in an
irrigation network. The community continued losing land until finally
it disappeared, giving way to a number of haciendas, among which
Siglo XX was the largest.

In the 1950s and 1960s, the descendents of the successful scissors
merchant transformed Siglo XX into a centrally managed agro-
industrial unit dedicated almost entirely to cotton production. On the
eve of land reform, the hacienda comprised 1,500 ha of land and
thirty-six irrigation wells supplied with electrical pumps. It also had
its own cotton gin, an electrical plant, and several workshops.
Because of the large size and agro-industrial character of the
hacienda, the composition of the labour force at Siglo XX was much
more heterogeneous than at Alamos (see Table 10). In 1972, Siglo XX
employed eighteen overseers and office clerks in addition to twenty
skilled workers (tractor and truck drivers, mechanics, electricians,
etc.). As for the unskilled labour force, it consisted of 260 stable field

labourers (some of whom were transferred to the gin after the harvest), 100 quasi-temporary labourers, and 500 cotton pickers. Most cotton pickers were recruited among migrants from the highlands, many of whom were illiterate or did not even speak Spanish.

The massive inflow of highland workers (*serranos*) complicated the internal structure of the hacienda. In effect, it consisted of three large administrative sectors, each with its own worker residential area. One sector, known as the factory, included the gin, electrical plant, workshops and administrative offices. The factory's labour force was made up of skilled workers and employees, mostly of local origin. The two other sectors were agricultural. One was situated close to the factory; its labour force was composed of both local and *serrano* workers. The second sector was   exclusively comprised of *serranos*. While the migrants from the Sierra tended to mix with the local labourers in the first agricultural sector, the *serranos* in the second sector formed a close community which succeeded in preserving its distinctive identity. After land reform, Siglo xx incorporated two other small centrally managed estates, which formed the third agricultural sector composed primarily of local labourers.

Siglo xx had the first rural union in the area. It was formed at the end of the 1950s by local *apristas*. In the late 1960s, the union leaders established contacts with the Communists and, after land reform was begun, the union became affiliated with the CGTP. Originally, the union included only the workers. In 1965, however, the hacienda employees, dissatisfied with their wages, organized a Committee for the Defence of the Employees. The Committee supported the workers' demands for wage increases and, in 1968, merged with the workers' union.

The labour union at Siglo xx was much more militant than the union at Alamos. During the 1960s and early 1970s, it conducted a number of strikes. The longest one (thirteen days) was provoked by the owners' decision to suspend seventeen stable field labourers. Shortly after these events, the owners divided the hacienda into five estates and sold them to some hacienda employees to avoid expropriation. The union leaders went to court, arguing that the transaction was illegal, and won the case. The actual expropriation of the hacienda took place only in 1972, three years after the promulgation of land reform and after another strike. Eleven years later, the co-operative workers were still proud of this episode: "How do you think we've made this co-operative? Some say: 'with clean hands.' That's not true. We've made it fighting. We went on strike [and] stayed a whole week without money: there was nothing to eat. Nobody could come in here because we had blocked the entrance. And inside, everything was run by the union. This is how we've made it, and not with clean hands!" (field labourer).

Even though Siglo XX's workers were actively involved in the expropriation of the hacienda, the major role in the co-operative was played by the state. Contrary to Alamos, Siglo XX was a typical state-sponsored co-operative. From 1972 to 1974 it was managed by the government-appointed Regional Administrative Committee. Later it was allowed to elect its own executive, but these were held responsible to the Ministry of Agriculture, SINAMOS, and Agrarian Bank. From the very start, Siglo XX enjoyed state financial support. The state also provided funds for compensation paid to the former hacienda owners.

The state-sponsored origin of the co-operative at Siglo XX accounted, to some extent, for the contradictory policies in its socio-economic organization. On the one hand, concern with the co-operative's economic efficiency made the Ministry of Agriculture refrain from radical changes in the hacienda occupational structure. At any rate, such changes would have been difficult to implement since, unlike Alamos, Siglo XX was not only a highly centralized, but also an industrialized hacienda. As a consequence, the hacienda occupational structure after land reform remained virtually unchanged. All the hacienda employees, except the manager, joined the co-operative, retaining their previous positions. On the other hand, access to generous state credit enabled the co-operative leadership to expand Siglo XX's stable labour force, granting co-operative membership (which, among other things, implied labour stability) to numerous quasi-temporary labourers (the stable labourers' relatives for the most part). Between 1972 and 1981, the size of the stable labour force at Siglo XX increased by half (from 300 to 450), while the cultivated areas over the same period increased by only 20 per cent (from 1,500 to 1,850 ha) (see Table 10). The growth of the stable labour force was especially noticeable at the factory. In 1981, it counted 150 employees and skilled workers as compared to only fifty in 1972 (see Table 12).

The increase in the skilled labour force after land reform could not be adequately explained by the co-operative's agro-industrial development. The technological level and operation of the factory did not dramatically change after land reform. The main reasons for change appeared to be social, rather than economic or technical. Work at at the factory was generally considered much more attractive — better paid, less demanding, and more prestigious — than work in the fields. The employees were still the best-paid occupational category in the co-operative. In addition to their regular wages, they enjoyed

TABLE 12: Composition of skilled labour force at Siglo xx, 1981

Department/occupation	Number
Supervisory staff	11
Disease control	8
Accounting	8
Payroll	11
Warehouse and marketing	7
Cotton gin	8
Electrical plant	7
Tractor drivers	24
Truck and car drivers	16
Mechanic shop	14
Irrigation infrastructure and lathes	18
Electrical shop	8
Carpentry	3
Printing shop	3
Watchmen	5
Other	6
Total	157

SOURCE: Co-operative accounts

numerous side benefits ranging from paid trips to Lima to the private use of co-operative funds. As for the factory's skilled workers, even though their regular wages were not much higher than those of the field labourers, their total income considerably exceeded the income of the latter. This was especially true for tractor drivers, truck or car drivers, well operators, and the electrical plant staff. All earned generous overtime calculated at special rates which raised their monthly incomes by forty to fifty per cent. Given these and the other attractions of factory jobs, numerous young field labourers with influential relatives or friends within the co-operative were transferred, year after year, from the field to the factory, inflating the overall number of the co-operative's skilled labour force.

The persistence of occupational inequalities combined with the growth of the skilled labour force caused profound discontent among co operative field labourers.

"Look at what's happening at the factory. Let's say something is wrong with a truck, so it has to be repaired. And the driver, what is he doing in the meanwhile? Sitting in the shadow, drinking his Coke, reading a newspaper. Why don't they give him a spade so that he could go and work with us in the field? It's all hypocrisy. Work, they say, we must work! Even Belaunde came here, waving a spade. But the only people who really toil are us, the field

TABLE 13: Real wages and salaries of co-operative members at Siglo XX, 1975-81 (in 1,000 *soles* in 1975 currency)*

	1975	1976	1977	1978	1979	1980	1981
Employees (average)	5,200	5,239	4,378	4,986	3,998	6,114	4,075
Skilled workers (average)	3,660	4,183	3,601	4,171	3,640	5,617	3,964
Field workers	3,150	3,437	3,288	3,575	3,350	5,435	3,819

SOURCE: Co-operative accounts
*Calculated on the basis of consumer price indexes provided by the Regional Branch of the Ministry of Agriculture

workers. All those who loiter at the factory, why don't they come out to work in the field? Why should we maintain them? You know how it is in a family: one son is working here, another there. If one has nothing to do, the father sends him to help the other. So it should also be in the cooperative, but it is not so." (field labourer)

The discontent with occupational inequalities made some of the field labourers propose, soon after the co-operativization, to equalize co-operative wages as Alamos had done. However, the proposal did not find much support. Instead, an agreement was reached to ask the Ministry of Agriculture for a wage increase and, after a year of negotiations, the Ministry granted a fifty per cent increase to the entire co-operative membership. This first increase opened the way for annual increases considerably exceeding those granted to its members by Alamos (see Table 11). The wage increases were particularly large for field labourers. Confronted with the egalitarian co-operative rhetoric on the one hand, and occupational inequalities on the other, they pressed for higher wages to match the incomes of the employees and skilled workers. The results of this pressure were quite amazing. By the early 1980s, the intraco-operative wage differentials had virtually levelled off. Moreover, throughout this period, the field labourers' real wages at Siglo XX climbed, despite national wage control policies and, later on, despite the co-operative's economic difficulties (see Table 13).

The same expansive logic could be seen in the co-operative's social policies. Apart from wages and salaries, the co-operative provided its members with multiple economic and social benefits. At the end of the financial year, it distributed dividends which, however, were only of minor importance in comparison with wages (see Table 11). The co-operative also provided its members with quotas of free food products from the co-operative fields and occasionally sold them other food-stuffs below market prices. In addition, co-operative members benefitted from interest-free personal loans far exceeding the loans Alamos granted to its members. In 1974, the co-operative, in co-ordination with SINAMOS, implemented a literacy campaign; it also hired a physician and a social worker for members. A new office complex was built and a civic centre started. The co-operative members were provided with working clothes paid for by the co-operative. The administration also organized sewing and cooking classes for women, having purchased all the necessary equipment for that purpose. In addition, it bought printing equipment and started to publish a co-operative bulletin entitled *The Truth*. Coupled with the wage increases, the social programs considerably improved the position of the field labourers, even though some programs were rather controversial and failed.[3]

The trend toward equalization in the distribution of these "formal" co-operative incomes and benefits was offset, however, by a counter-trend toward socio-economic differentiation because of private economic activities conducted contrary to the production co-operative regulations. This second trend was facilitated, to some extent, by a deteriorating internal management following the co-operativization of the hacienda. Before land reform, labour discipline was enforced by the overseers, exclusively responsible to the manager and the owners of the hacienda. In practice, they had almost unlimited power over the labourers, a power which they frequently used in an arbitrary, abusive way. The situation changed after land reform, when the supervisory staff became responsible to the General Assembly, as was also the case at Alamos. However, the new system of authority did not work the same way at Alamos and Siglo XX. At Alamos, the supervisors, elected from the ranks of field labourers and subject to new elections every year, acquired a new co-operative legitimacy in the eyes of their subordinates. At Siglo XX, by contrast, the supervisors remained unchanged from pre-reform times: the same overseers who had been hated for their abuses before land reform were still overseers ten years later. However, during the same time, they lost much of their original power. They could no longer fire, suspend, or mistreat workers, as they had been allowed to do by the former owners. In fact, they could hardly use any sanctions at all: workers whom they attempted to discipline promptly took their cases to the General Assembly and the sanctions were inevitably cancelled by the sympathetic worker majority. According to some informants, mostly overseers and other employees, this situation resulted in a considerable deterioration of individual field labourers' work.

"People just don't want to work as they used to. There are many loafers here, and not at the factory; there, at least, they work until 5 p.m. It's in the field sectors. They should work there to 12, but sometimes you go to check at 8:30 or 9, and there is nobody around. As soon as it starts getting hot, they go home, without bothering about finishing their task. If you ask me, this is the land reform officials' fault. They used to come here and say to the peasants: 'You are the owners now, the land is yours.' Very well! But that was the end of respect for the overseers." (overseer)

While it is plausible to suggest that the problem of labour discipline was exaggerated and dramatized by the resentful overseers, their accusations seemed to contain some truth. Ironically, many found it easier to co-operate with sluggish field labourers than to persist in maintaining work standards. The permissiveness of the supervisory staff reached such a degree that in 1980 the co-operative decided to shift the overseers from one field sector to another to prevent the supervisors and the supervised from coming to mutually suitable agreements.[4]

Most field labourers used the relaxed labour regulations to expand their private economic activities, trying to increase their co-operative incomes. Contrary to co-operative regulations, some preserved plots outside the co-operative, to which they devoted part of their time. In addition, virtually all co-operative members, and field labourers in particular, raised cattle, a practice prohibited by former hacienda owners but permitted by the co-operative administration.[5]

The search for additional incomes was also desperate among the skilled workers. They, however, had an eight-hour working day, which left them with practically no time for work outside the factory. Moreover, they depended on the factory facilities: machines and instruments, warehouse materials, and fuel for their economic activities. Nevertheless, the deteriorating management system affected them no less than the field labourers, albeit in a different way: they learned to stretch their overtime, to obtain a large number of private orders, and to pilfer co-operative property — all with the tacit consent of their supervisors. However, it was the supervisors, together with the manager and the senior office clerks who were able to manipulate the co-operative economy most effectively for their own benefit.

According to co-operative statutes, co-operative employees were accountable to the manager who was, in turn, accountable to the General Assembly. However, the Assembly's control over administration at Siglo XX was illusionary (see Chapter 5). Not surprisingly, many co-operative employees took advantage of this situation to further their own interests. Financial scandals became routine at Siglo XX. During the ten years of its existence, the co-operative conducted three audits at the request of its members. All three discovered serious financial irregularities involving the manager, the senior employees, and the members of the Administrative Council. Curiously, no senior employees were expelled. Moreover, most kept their jobs even after sensational revelations.

Corruption augmented the incomes of senior co-operative employees, enabling them to invest in land or small businesses (usually trade or repair services). In addition, some succeeded in appropriating, de facto, portions of co-operative land unsuitable for mechanized large-scale production. Accordingly, their dependence on co-operative incomes diminished, while their capacity to engage in lucrative private activities outside the co-operative rose. In this way, they also preserved or even increased the social and economic distance separating them from the field labourers.

Clearly, the post-reform situation at Siglo XX contrasted with that at Alamos. From the pre-reform period, Siglo XX inherited an extremely diversified occupational structure. The occupational inequalities constituted a permanent source of internal tension and caused the members of the "unprivileged" group, the field labourers, to press for improvements in their position vis-à-vis the employees and the skilled workers. Substantial wage increases and vast social programs were partly a response of the co-operative administration to this pressure. However, they were also encouraged by the extensive government support which the co-operative enjoyed from the time it was formed. The expansive wage and social policies considerably improved the members' standards of living. However, this improvement was marred by the socio-economic differentiation among the co-operative members resulting from economic activities. While the field workers looked for meagre complementary incomes by cultivating plots or breeding livestock, the equally modest ventures of the skilled workers continued to be attached to the co-operative infrastructure. As for the major beneficiaries of this process, the co-operative employees, they originally derived most of their additional revenues from the co-operative. However, as their private fortunes grew, they started to detach from co-operative sources of income and to invest in land and businesses.

MONTE BLANCO:
STATE-SPONSORED CO-OPERATIVE
ON A DECENTRALIZED HACIENDA

Like Siglo XX, Monte Blanco was co-operativized under the state-sponsored land reform. However, in contrast to Siglo XX, Monte Blanco had never had much political or economic weight. Its pre-reform history is obscure and controversial. In the late 1930s and 1940s it was owned by a mysterious landlord who, as the story runs, had won it playing cards with another local landowner. None of the local informants knew him personally and none could say for sure where he lived (some believed in Spain).

The hacienda was divided into three independent sectors: Upper, Central, and Lower Monte Blanco, with 300, 70, and 350 ha respectively. All three were rented to different local landowners who, for all practical purposes, were considered the owners of the hacienda. These landowners subdivided most of their lands into plots and rented them to small tenants.

The situation changed in the 1950s when Anderson Clayton started to drill wells in the vicinity of Monte Blanco. As water for irrigation became permanently available the big renters ("owners") of the hacienda attempted to introduce direct cotton production. The attempt, however, was not entirely successful. Ten years later the wells started to dry up; consequently, the hacienda had to return to the system of tenancy. On the eve of land reform, only one sector, Lower Monte Blanco, still had a relatively large centralized area. In the central sector, this area was insignificant and in Upper Monte Blanco it did not exist at all; because of the acute and chronic shortage of water, the lands there were either abandoned or taken over, in fact, if not by law, by small tenants.

The hacienda's stable labour force was tiny. Upper Monte Blanco had no stable workers at all. Central Monte Blanco had twelve stable field labourers and one field supervisor. Even the relatively highly centralized lower sector had only twenty-one stable workers (five skilled) and four employees. Most agricultural operations in the centrally managed areas of both sectors were performed by quasi-temporary labourers: between fifty and sixty of them worked on the hacienda for most of the year.

In the mid-1960s, the twenty-one stable workers of Lower Monte Blanco unionized. This union, however, was not as active as the union at Siglo XX or even as the one at Alamos. Its main achievement appears to have been the management's construction of barracks for the hacienda's manual labourers. Shortly after land reform, the union wrote the Ministry of Agriculture requesting the expropriation and co-operativization of its sector of the hacienda. The request was granted. However, in accordance with the ministerial resolution, the co-operative was to include not only Lower Monte Blanco, but also both other sectors of the hacienda plus two other estates (one 150 ha and one 42 ha, each with a few stable labourers).

From the very beginning, co-operativization presented certain difficulties. To obtain co-operative membership, the hacienda's tenants had to surrender title of their plots to the co-operative. Many did so, expecting that work in the co-operative would bring them more economic benefits than would the ownership of a plot. The actual benefits, however, proved to be less than expected. The disillusionment was especially bitter among former tenants of Upper Monte Blanco: they believed that the co-operative wages ratified by the Ministry of Agriculture were ludicrously low. After several months of attempts to obtain a wage increase, they withdrew their memberships and their plots from the co-operative and formed an independent service co-operative. Some former tenants in other sectors followed suit. As a consequence, in May 1973, the co-operative was reorganized. Its area shrank from 900 ha to 600 ha; membership fell from 120 to 90. In addition to the land, the co-operative had for assets around ten irrigation wells, most in very poor condition, and four tractors.

As already mentioned, only twenty-one out of ninety co-operative members had been unionized stable workers. The remainder were quasi-temporary or unorganized stable workers and small tenants. Most hacienda employees joined the co-operative, even though they had never had good relations with the union. In actual fact, the hacienda labour force's participation in land reform was minimal. By and large, co-operative members had neither organizational experience, nor, indeed, much interest in forming the co-operative.

Organized by the state from an expropriated hacienda, Monte Blanco shared many important characteristics with Siglo XX. The occupational structure at Monte Blanco was basically similar to that at Siglo XX (see Table 10). The number of skilled workers at Monte Blanco grew faster than the number of field labourers, although not as fast as at Siglo XX. Moreover, this growth was at least partly supported by the expansion of the co-operative irrigation infrastructure and machine pool caused by the switch from tenancy to direct cultivation tenancy after land reform. Almost half of the co-operative skilled workers at Monte Blanco were tractor drivers and well operators (see Table 14).

Skilled jobs at Monte Blanco had the same attraction for co-operative members as they had at Siglo XX: not only were these jobs better paid, but they also provided workers with additional material and non-material benefits. Nevertheless, Monte Blanco succeeded in curbing the number of skilled workers much better than Siglo XX. Thus, promotions at Monte Blanco usually had to be approved by the General Assembly. In addition, at least during the initial years, those field labourers who replaced skilled workers had to reassume their work in the field and their normal wages as soon as the skilled workers in question returned to their duties. Even more important, Monte

TABLE 14: Composition of skilled labour force at Monte Blanco, 1980

Department/occupation	Number of workers
Supervisory	4
Disease control	1
Accounting and payroll	7
Warehouse	2
Tractor drivers	7
Truck and car drivers	3
Well operators	7
Mechanics	1
Other	1
Total	33

SOURCE: Co-operative accounts

Blanco, unlike Siglo XX, adopted a rather restrictive membership policy, thereby reducing pressure for promotions. When the co-operative was formed in 1973, membership was extended to some hacienda quasi-temporary labourers, all heads of families. Later, however, practically no others were admitted. Moreover, in 1978 the co-operative prohibited replacing retiring members by their relatives — a usual practice in most other co-operatives. In 1979 and 1980, the General Assembly considered several petitions from retiring members seeking admission for their children who worked in the co-operative on a quasi-temporary basis. The answer was inevitably no: "They should continue working as temporary labourers provided that there is any work at all" (Book of Records 1979). As a consequence, co-operative membership declined from 118 in 1976 to 96 in 1981. Another consequence was a relatively low proportion of younger, better educated members who, in Siglo XX, filled junior administrative positions at the factory.

Even if the growth of skilled labour force at Monte Blanco was not as explosive as it was at Siglo XX, the skilled personnel's relations with the field labourers were far from consensual. The employees' and skilled workers' higher wages for duties generally viewed as easy by most field labourers was a permanent source of discontent. When the Ministry of Agriculture ratified 50 per cent wage increases for all co-operative personnel in 1974, they were bitterly opposed by the field labourers. A good part of this opposition was due to the simultaneous extension of the field working day from five to eight hours, but the injustice of giving the employees what appeared to the field labourers to be a disproportionate, undeserved increase played a major role in raising their discontent, as the following excerpt from the co-operative

General Assembly record illustrates:

The presentation of the deputy [of the Ministry of Agriculture, concerning the wage increase] is interrupted, unpolitely, by cooperative members M.C. and M.T. [both field workers] who say that they do not know how much the employees earn. The deputy answers their question, after which members F.H. and T.H. [also field workers] express their opinion that, in this case, it is better not to have any increases at all, and that employees spend their working hours having a good time in the town. After this, member M.C. intervenes once again, saying that in the co-operative there are many loafers, a word which hurts everybody present. He is also asking why there are three or four operators for each well [when only one is really needed] . . . . [Finally], the Assembly starts to insist that there should be no wage increases at all and that the working day in the field should remain five hours, as before. The deputy explains that the personnel must change their mentality, adding that other-wise the cooperative may have problems, because the government will cer-tainly take measures. His words are followed by a silence. Then, member A.C. says: "why don't we divide the land and work individually?" To this the deputy responds: "That, never!" After this, the secretary reads the ministe-rial resolution establishing wage increases for the co-operative of Monte Blanco. (Book of Records 9 August 1974)

The 50 per cent wage increase for the entire membership, as well as the eight-hour working day, was unwillingly ratified by the General Assembly. The second provision, however, proved to be difficult to implement: several months later, the co-operative returned to the habitual five-hour working day. As expected, this did not affect the new wages. The first wage increase was followed by annual increases considerably exceeding those established in Alamos and close to those granted by Siglo XX. These increases primarily benefitted the co-operative field labourers whose real wages climbed, while the wages and salaries of the skilled labour force tended to stagnate or even decline (see Table 15). The social programs at Monte Blanco were also quite ambitious. Before land reform, Monte Blanco had no access to public services available to the two other haciendas. It had no medical or school facilities, and public transportation was almost non-existent. Encouraged by the land reform officials, the co-operative established its own medical centre and an elementary school, paying a doctor and two teachers from co-operative funds. The co-operative also opened a grocery store for its members, selling foodstuffs and some consumer goods brought from the nearby town in a co-operative truck.

In other words, Monte Blanco made an attempt to diminish intra-

TABLE 15: Real wages and salaries of co-operative members, Monte Blanco, 1975-81 (per 1,000 *soles* in 1975 currency)*

	1975	1976	1977	1978	1979	1980	1981
Employees (average)	4,830	5,089	4,391	4,197	3,814	—	3,679
Skilled workers	3,300	3,730	3,509	3,672	3,269	—	3,372
Field workers	2,700	3,197	3,105	3,405	3,068	—	3,264

SOURCE: Co-operative accounts
*Calculated on the basis of consumer price indexes provided by The Regional Branch of the Ministry of Agriculture.

co-operative social and economic inequalities like Siglo XX. And, as at Siglo XX, this attempt largely failed because of a countertrend toward socio-economic differentiation in private economic activities, accompanied by declining individual work performance as pronounced as it was at Siglo XX:

"Personal productivity is getting lower every year. When the co-operative was just formed, people worked well. We had a five-hour task, like now, but it was a big task. Then, little by little, they started to relax. This, I think, was the fault of the land reform officials. They used to come here and say: 'you are the owners of this land, you are the *patrones* now.' And if somebody believes he is a *patrón*, do you think he is going to work? So the cooperative started to hire more and more [quasi-]temporary labourers. Last year, we had forty of them, working all year long. And there was always some work for members' wives and children." (assistant agronomist)

As at Siglo XX, the informants might have exaggerated the problem. Monte Blanco's increased use of quasi-temporary labour could also be explained by the co-operative's greater cultivated area (from 1975 to 1981 it increased by more than 200 ha while the number of co-operative field labourers remained virtually the same). Still, a gradual reduction of the working day seemed to become as habitual at Monte Blanco as it had at Siglo XX.

The field labourers dedicated the time left over from their work in the co-operative to tending their plots and raising cattle. The amount of livestock at Monte Blanco far exceeded that at Siglo XX. The scope of private cattle raising is indirectly revealed by repeated, and apparently never implemented, decisions of the General Assembly to fine the owners of cattle found in the fields. Family agriculture at Monte Blanco was also more important than at Siglo XX. As already mentioned, the hacienda practised the system of tenancy prior to land reform. After co-operativization, those tenants who wanted to join the co-operative had to give up their plots to the co-operative. Many, however, obtained co-operative membership without surrendering their land. Although some were later expelled, there are good reasons to believe that, despite co-operative purges, many held onto their plots, contrary to co-operative regulations.

The persistence of family agriculture after the decentralized part of the hacienda was incorporated into the centrally managed production unit could be explained, to a large extent, by the peculiarities of Monte Blanco's irrigation infrastructure. To repeat, the irrigation well system on the pre-reform hacienda was rather deficient. After land reform, the co-operative built several new wells and expanded the centralized cotton production. Nevertheless, family agriculture survived in the peripheral, poorly irrigated co-operative areas. At the same time, the hacienda had direct access to the local river. Even though water supply from the river was quite limited, it substituted for subterranean water on some co-operative fields. These fields where irrigation did not depend on the well system controlled by the co-operative also became informally privatized.

While the field labourers' complementary activities were largely limited to work on plots inside or outside the co-operative boundaries, some of the technical-administrative staff operated lucrative sidelines using co-operative resources. The records of General Assemblies and interviews with co-operative members reveal that corruption among employees was as common at Monte Blanco as it was at Siglo XX. While its impact upon the co-operative economy was probably exaggerated by informants, corruption certainly provided some employees with considerable revenues. Although conclusive evidence is not available, it seems plausible to suggest that at Monte Blanco, as at Siglo XX, these revenues were channeled into purchases of land or into small businesses.

CONCLUSION

The three co-operatives selected for case studies differed considerably in origin and pre-reform experiences. Two, Siglo XX and Monte Blanco, had been organized by the Ministry of Agriculture from expropriated haciendas, as part of the state-sponsored co-operative network. One, Alamos, had been formed independently by the workers who had bought the hacienda directly from its owners.

Production on the pre-reform haciendas was also different. All three were capitalist cotton haciendas relying on seasonal migrant labour. In this sense, their operation reflected a functional dualism between the coastal/highland and the highland/peasant sectors (see

Chapter 2). Siglo XX and Monte Blanco also depended on the local peasant sector where they recruited their local quasi-temporary labourers. The co-operativization of the haciendas did not change the coastal/highland functional dualism. However, Siglo XX and, to a lesser extent, Monte Blanco extended the co-operative membership to many of their local quasi-temporary labourers. This measure suggests that the impact of the land reform and co-operativization was not, after all, as limited as suggested in Chapter 2. Even if the conversion of cotton estates into co-operatives did not bring change in their relations with the highland peasantry, it still extended co-operative benefits to a considerable number of local quasi-temporary labourers. This extension does not seem to be sufficiently significant to change the position of the local smallholding sector as a whole. Nevertheless, it was large enough to affect the co-operatives. The incorporation of the quasi-temporary labourers expanded the haciendas' stable labour force, which, at least at Siglo XX, was not supported by a similar increase in the co-operatives' production capacity.

To the differences in the size of the co-operatives' memberships (as related to their productive capacity), I add the differences in their socio-economic organization. The independent, socially homogeneous Alamos adopted a co-operative model based on organizational autonomy and internal equality. As a result, it had an astoundingly low level of occupational and income differentiation deliberately kept in check by the co-operative field labourers which, of course, caused a certain discontent among the co-operative skilled workers. Nevertheless, the low level of differentiation prevented deeper antagonisms between the "privileged" and "unprivileged" occupational groups and made co-operative field labourers accept wages and hours otherwise deemed unacceptable. Moreover, since Alamos was formed without state support, its members adopted a rather cautious position on co-operative spending in general. The same lack of state support made them feel primarily responsible for the success of their enterprise. This perception, combined with a feeling of internal solidarity, resulted in a highly satisfactory work performance, at least until the early 1980s, when the decline in the workers' incomes motivated them to look for other income. However, private economic activities in Alamos seemed to be rather modest, in comparison to both state-sponsored co-operatives. Moreover, these activities were not related to internal corruption, partly because the group most amenable to it, the employees, was virtually non-existent, and partly because of efficient internal administrative controls (see Chapter 5).

The situation in both state-sponsored co-operatives was almost the

opposite. These co-operatives maintained the pre-reform occupational structure yet came under state administration controls, which
were not, however, very effective. The purpose of state controls was to
preserve or improve the economic efficiency of expropriated haciendas to increase their contribution to import-substitution industrialization (see Chapter 2). Accordingly, these controls were designed to
impose restraints on co-operative wage and social expenses, to guarantee efficient management, and to enforce labour discipline. In both
state-sponsored co-operatives, however, these objectives remained
largely unfulfilled. The hacienda workers apparently turned state
intervention in co-operativization to their advantage, at least in some
important respects. The workers of the state-sponsored Siglo XX and
Monte Blanco received higher wages and had better social services
than did their counterparts at the independent Alamos. Many also
obtained labour stability which they did not have before the land
reform. Moreover, Siglo XX practised expansive promotion policies
permitting many field labourers to obtain skilled jobs. The improvements in workers' positions were accompanied, however, by socio-
economic differentiation in private economic activities which
primarily benefitted the co-operative employees. The growth of these
activities accounted for pronounced income inequalities in both state-
sponsored co-operatives. It also implied the deterioration of individual work performance discussed earlier in Chapter 2. I argued then
that poor individual work performance after land reform could be
explained by the lack of co-operativist commitment among members,
and that it was rooted in the state-dependent origins of the co-
operative movement. While the experiences of Alamos diverging
from those of Siglo XX and Monte Blanco seem to confirm this argument, it still needs certain qualifications.

The effect of state intervention on individual work performance in
post-reform co-operatives seems to have been mediated by the development of private economic activities which absorbed much of the
members' time and energy. Moreover, this development not only
affected the members' performance, but also informally privatized the
co-operative economy which, as I shall show later, constituted a prel-
ude for the formal privatization involved in the subdivision of co-
operative lands. At the same time, state controls did not prevent the
hacienda workers from obtaining tangible socio-economic benefits,
such as labour stability, wages, and social services. As a consequence,
while failing to develop a genuine co-operativist commitment, workers could still feel committed to the existing co-operative organization
with all its shortcomings. As I shall also show later, this "pragmatic"

commitment was one reason for their opposition to subdividing co-operative lands which, if carried out, would deprive them of the protective co-operative umbrella.

With these qualifications, the argument about the negative effect of state intervention on members' co-operativist commitment and individual work performance still seems valid. This effect in the state-sponsored co-operatives was amplified by the misfunctioning of the co-operative institutions, discussed in Chapter 5.

CHAPTER FIVE

Co-Operative Institutions: Internal Participation and External Political Involvement

The conversion of the three cotton haciendas to production co-operatives had mixed socio-economic results. Only small and politically independent Alamos achieved a high level of social equity and satisfactory individual work performance. The large state-sponsored co-operatives, Siglo XX and Monte Blanco, became characterized by pronounced internal inequalities, mismanagement, and deterioration of discipline among labourers.

These undesirable phenomena should have been kept in check by the co-operative institutions designed to guarantee worker participation in co-operative administration. According to co-operative statutes approved by the Ministry of Agriculture, the supreme authority in production co-operatives was the General Assembly. It met at least twice a year for making major economic decisions — such as the ratification of financial accounts and production plans — and for electing the Administrative Council and the Supervisory Council. The Assembly also elected committees for dealing with specific co-operative issues (marketing, education, social security, etc.). These committees, as well as the Supervisory Council, played only a minor role, however, in comparison with its Administrative Council whose members, along with its employees, managed the co-operative on a daily basis (see Appendices 1-3).

In many cases, the co-operative institutions co-existed with pre-reform labour unions. In principle, the unions were supposed to become obsolete after the transformation of haciendas into co-operatives. In practice, however, the inadequate functioning of the co-operative institutions frequently led to the continuation of unionist activities within the co-operative framework. The co-operative labour unions constituted an additional mechanism of worker participation in management, channelling workers' demands and supervising co-operative authorities.

The co-operative institutions also provided for the members' participation in national politics, under the inclusionary-corporatist rules of the game (see Chapter 2). The state-sponsored co-operatives became affiliated with the Agrarian Leagues and federations forming the National Agrarian Confederation (CNA) and supervised by the National System of Support for Social Mobilization (SINAMOS). They also joined the CNA-sponsored Central Co-operatives and the Committees of Agricultural Producers. After the inclusionary-corporatist framework collapsed in 1975, and the CNA was transformed into a political opposition force, the co-operatives continued their affiliation with this organization, participating more or less enthusiastically in its political undertakings (see Chapter 3). Below, I examine the internal operation of the co-operative institutions and their relations with the national co-operative movement, focusing on the differences between the state-sponsored and the independent co-operatives.

ALAMOS: CO-OPERATIVE DEMOCRACY

An effective co-operative democracy accompanied the radical transformation of the occupational structure at Alamos described in Chapter 4. The workers at Alamos had become deeply involved in co-operative decisionmaking. In 1982, the co-operative had sixty members, and thirty-two, more than half, had served on the Administrative Council (elected at Alamos for a one-year period). Fourteen out of these thirty-two had been elected only once; eighteen others had served for two or more years, forming what could be considered a relatively stable elected co-operative leadership. Fourteen out of the eighteen re-elected leaders were field labourers. The other four were co-operative skilled workers. Field labourers at Alamos were also most likely to hold the presidency in the Administrative Council. During the thirteen years of its existence, the co-operative had twelve presidents, eight of whom were field labourers.

Thus, the occupational composition of the elected leadership at Alamos closely reflected the co-operative's occupational structure: it was essentially a field labourers' leadership. Those who were underrepresented on the Administrative Council were not an occupational, but an age group: the younger co-operative workers. Co-operative leaders were recruited among older hacienda workers — "the founding fathers," as the young members called them, half respectfully, half mockingly. Only four of the eighteen re-elected leaders and only one of the twelve presidents were under thirty. This situation caused a certain discontent among the younger workers, who, by 1982, constituted almost half of the membership. But as their numbers grew, so did their electoral strength. In 1982, for the first time in the co-operative's history, younger workers gained control of the Administrative Council. They won four out of five Council positions, including the presidency.

The co-operative councils at Alamos were closely supervised by the General Assembly:

"Everything here is decided by the General Assembly. Our councils are not autonomous as they are in other cooperatives. . . . To be sure, the Administrative Council has a right to make some decisions, but usually they don't even want to use this right. They prefer to take all problematic questions to the Assembly. That's because they are afraid: what if they make a decision [without consulting the Assembly] and something goes wrong!" (tractor driver)

Initially, the General Assembly met monthly; later, it started to meet twice a month or even more frequently. Thus, during the first two years of the co-operative's existence from 1970 to 1971, the co-operative held twenty-two general assemblies; ten years later, during 1980 and 1981, it held forty-seven.

According to the co-operative's Books of Records, the assemblies had a distinctively technical character. All started with reports by the supervisory and technical staff, followed by a broad general discussion. Because of the incomplete character of the records, it is impossible to quantitatively evaluate the members' participation in discussions. What can be evaluated is membership participation through the presentation of oral requests to the General Assembly. Such requests could vary widely from a request for some personal benefit to a call for the resignation of the co-operative councils. All, however, represented attempts to influence co-operative decisionmaking. This form of participation at Alamos had been growing constantly. During 1970 and 1971, thirteen out of twenty-two co-operative assemblies included requests from individual members. Their total number amounted to 114. Half of the requests came from co-operative employees, the other half, from skilled workers and field labourers. The situation had changed, and considerably so, ten years later. During 1980 and 1981, twenty-eight out of the forty-seven assemblies included requests. The total number of requests remained approximately the same: 110. However, only six (5 per cent) were made by the manager — the only remaining employee; thirty-four requests (30 per cent) were made by skilled workers, and seventy (64 per cent) by field labourers.

The analysis of the occupational background of the elected leadership and the changing patterns of requests suggest that worker participation at Alamos was rather effective. Another indicator was a successful struggle against corruption among the elected co-operative leadership.

The first case of corruption — a "loss" of co-operative money — was reported in 1977, eight years after the co-operative began. The General Assembly forced the implicated leader to return the money and added the following provision to the co-operative regulations: "Starting from this date on, if some co-operative leader or member loses co-operative money, he should become financially responsible for this loss, unless he was assaulted either with knives or with other weapons" (Book of Records 1977). The same year, however, the president of the Administrative Council spent more money than he had been allowed by the General Assembly during his trip to Lima. The sum was relatively insignificant — 1,700 *soles*, a co-operative worker's weekly wages. The co-operative's reaction, nevertheless, was surprisingly harsh. The president was subjected to an exemplary trial. He was forced not only to make restitution under the new rule, but also to resign as president. Moreover, he was banned from holding any administrative position in the future. In explanation of this harshness, the General Assembly made the following statement signed by all members: "We point out that this attitude is due not to the amount of money spent by President H.C. contrary to the permission of the Assembly, but to the very fact of his doing so. This attitude should remain as a precedent for all future presidents and other leaders who will have the management of the co-operative in their hands" (Book of Records, 7 May 1977).

The Book of Records mentions two other cases of corruption among council members, dealt with in more or less the same way. The General Assembly's ban on the members guilty of corruption was cancelled in 1980, on the pretext of the national general amnesty declared that year by President Belaunde. The "co-operative amnesty," as it became known among the membership, apparently did not affect the Assembly's power to control the councils.

The general satisfaction with the internal system of participation at Alamos was reflected in workers' organizational attitudes. During interviews at Alamos, all respondents except one agreed that general assemblies were absolutely necessary for the efficient administration of the co-operative economy, usually mentioning the diffusion of information about the economic and financial situation in the co-operative, public discussion, and collective decisionmaking. The performance of all three functions was viewed as highly satisfactory. Accordingly, no informant felt a need for a labour union in the co-operative. "What shall we want a union for? To defend us against whom? Against ourselves?," many respondents asked with genuine surprise. In fact, the workers' union was dissolved upon an agreement of its members soon after the hacienda had been transformed into a co-operative.

While worker participation in management at Alamos was definitely a success, its participation in the national co-operative movement was not. Having been created outside the legal framework of land reform, the Alamos co-operative deliberately avoided political contacts with SINAMOS, whose presence had been quite noticeable in other co-operatives. At the same time, it took advantage of most training programs organized by government agencies for co-operative members.[1] Alamos also became a member of the regional Central Co-operative. It seemed to be especially interested in the free accounting services which this organization offered to its members. Until 1974, Alamos contracted its own part-time accountant, whose salary was a permanent source of internal discord. Finally, the accountant was fired, and the co-operative started to use the Central Co-operative's accounting services. Alamos' relations with the Central Co-operative's political leadership, though, remained strained. In 1978, Alamos reached the extreme of withdrawing its membership, discontented with repeated financial scandals and internal strife which were eroding the Central Co-operative.

Alamos had also joined the CNA's local organization — the Agrarian League, even though it treated the league with even more reserve than the Central Co-operative. Initially, the relations between Alamos and the League seemed to be relatively good: Alamos participated in a radio program and in a university education scheme for co-operative members sponsored by the League, and sent its representatives to some regional meetings and conferences. Relations started to deteriorate in 1978, when the CNA lost government support and moved into political opposition. The CNA's anti-governmental stance did not find much response at Alamos. In the early 1980s, Alamos withdrew its membership from the CNA twice, arguing that the League "made politics instead of helping co-operatives." Disapproval of the CNA's and League's political activities was particularly strong among the older co-operative leaders. In 1980, for example, during the annual election of delegates to the League, the two proposed candidates (both older) withdrew their candidacies, raising a controversy around the League's political role in the valley. Eventually two younger workers were elected. Their involvement in regional politics, however, continued to be questioned inside the co-operative. When, in 1981, the League requested the co-operative's permission for one of Alamos' delegates to act temporarily as the League's president, the Administrative Council responded acidly that "the member in question will not be able to assume this responsibility, because there is much work to be done in the fields" (Book of Records, 13 July 1981).

The controversy surrounding Alamos' participation in the Agrarian League reflected the members' mistrust of the national co-operative movement. As a matter of fact, most respondents viewed the higher-level organizations as inefficient and over-politicized. The indifferent or negative attitudes toward the co-operative movement seemed to be related to Alamos' independent origins as well as to its astonishing success as a co-operative. They might also have certain political underpinnings. From the moment the hacienda union was organized to the present, most of the workers at Alamos supported APRA, a party opposed to the military government's land reform. Recently, however, APRA's influence has been challenged by the Socialist Revolutionary Party (PSR), a party organized by Velasco's followers after the fall of his government. The PSR established contacts with some younger workers questioning older co-operative leadership. In fact, the change in the age composition of the Administrative Council discussed earlier might lead to a change in the co-operative's political orientation and to its deeper involvement in regional and national politics.

In sum, after the co-operativization of the hacienda, Alamos was effectively run by its field labourers. Worker participation in management was facilitated by four interrelated factors: the small size and relatively simple organization of the hacienda; the adequate educational and organizational experience of its members; the practical non-existence of employees; and relative autonomy from the local state bureaucracies. Alamos involved itself in many training programs, which increased the administrative efficiency of its members, but it remained distinctively aloof from the more politically oriented activities. This aloofness could be partly explained by the peculiarity of Alamos' birth as a co-operative. However, another important factor was the *aprista* self-identification of its members, who were unwilling to become strongly involved in the co-operative movement controlled first by the Velasco government and later by the PSR.

SIGLO XX: BUREAUCRATIZATION AND POLITICIZATION OF CO-OPERATIVE INSTITUTIONS

Participation at Siglo XX and Monte Blanco was quite different from that at Alamos. At Siglo XX, only 45 out of 453 members (10 per cent) had served on the Administrative Council elected, as at Alamos, for a one-year period. Sixteen of these forty-five had been re-elected two or more times, and only six of these sixteen were manual workers: five field labourers and one skilled worker. Ten other re-elected leaders were factory employees, that is, they had already been involved in co-operative administration because of their occupation.

Clearly, in contrast to Alamos, the elected co-operative leadership in Siglo xx was dominated by the skilled labour force in general, and by the employees in particular. This could have several explanations. First, in a large, complex co-operative such as Siglo xx, field labourers were likely perceived by their fellow workers as unsuitable candidates for administrative positions. In addition, the factory staff controlled the allocation of resources within the co-operative, which certainly helped them to build electoral support among the field labourers. Finally, the field labourers were never able to present a single list of candidates as opposed to the single factory list. As already mentioned, the co-operative's fields were divided into three sectors. During elections, each sector presented its own candidate or list of candidates. This, of course, was not the best electoral strategy: in 1981, the factory sector had 157 members, while the three field sectors had 150, 126, and 20 members respectively. Nevertheless, intersectoral animosities prevented an electoral agreement among the field labourers. As already noted, one sector was situated near the factory. As a consequence, many of its members could develop close contacts with the factory staff, which certainly did not contribute to members of this sector understanding members of the two remote sectors. As for the remote sectors, each constituted a rather closed working and residential community, with its own identity and traditions. One was composed entirely of migrants from the Sierra; the other had been formed by independent estates incorporated into Siglo xx after land reform and was worked exclusively by local labourers.

Even more important than the employees' domination of the Administrative Council was the co-opting of many elected worker-leaders by the inner co-operative administration, frequently referred to as the "mafia." This was partly due to the manual labourers' lack of administrative experience, which meant that they were usually elected to low-ranking positions on the Council, known as *suplentes*, with the right of voice, but not of vote. By contrast, the positions of *titulares*, with voice and vote, and above all the dominant position of president, generally fell either to employees, or, less frequently, to skilled labourers. Thus, during the eleven years of its existence, Siglo xx had nine presidents, five of whom were co-operative employees (two held this position more than once). Three others were skilled workers, and only one was a field worker.[2]

The field labourers' failure to control the co-operative elected leadership added to their discontent with the occupational and income differences (discussed in Chapter 4), and created a rather strong antifactory feeling among them. The factory in general, and the elected factory leaders in particular, came to be viewed by many field labourers as largely responsible for the economic difficulties experienced by the co-operative. The following opinion, no matter how shocking it may sound, is representative of their attitudes toward the co-operative administration:

"When the co-operative was just formed, we were much better off. Why? I'll tell you why. Because the leaders here are a gang of thieves. . . . The only thing these gentlemen know is how to steal. . . . The cooperative had many things, the former owners left everything as it was: water pumps, tractors, the gin. But those who took it over did not use it well. They just stuffed themselves with money, they bought cars, they built houses, they had two or three women: one here, another there. Tell me, how can it be, if they earn as much as we do? Look, I have this hut, I have this wife of mine, and that's all. And I can hardly make ends meet. If I have a couple of beers, I feel bad about it. And those people get drunk every day. . . . The only president who really cared about the co-operative was S. and, mind you, he was the only one who came from the field. . . . The factory always get their people elected as presidents. . . . And, look, how many of them are now? 150, I believe. With the *patrón* there were only fifty, and all of them had to work. . . . And now nobody is doing anything. If you go to the factory, you will see it right away. One doesn't have to have an education to understand that much. In this co-operative, the clever ones [*sabios*] live off the fools [*sonzos*]. They sit at their desks and we till the land." (field labourer)

The sense of frustration among the field labourers was caused not only by most important positions on the Council being held by the factory staff, but also by the labourers' inability to control Council members through the General Assembly. The interviews conducted in the co-operative suggest that a large number of co-operative members, field labourers for the most part, did not perceive themselves as well equipped for meaningful participation in the discussions of the co-operative's complicated financial and economic affairs. Such participation would have required a minimal education and certain organizational experience. Many field labourers at Siglo XX lacked both. As already noted, many had been recruited among the nonunionized and illiterate quasi-temporary labourers. These relatively inexperienced members had little willingness or ability to become involved in co-operative administrative affairs.

As a consequence, a considerable number of Siglo XX's members had a very poor opinion of the General Assembly. Twenty-four out of fifty-four respondents (one-third of the interviewed employees and almost half of the workers) said that the general assemblies were totally useless. Even among those who believed that such meetings were necessary, the majority (twenty-five out of thirty) were sceptical about their effectiveness in decisionmaking, arguing that Assemblies were useful only as an arena for public debate or as a source of information. Moreover, the information obtained from assemblies was viewed by many of them as not entirely reliable: "Of course they [the assemblies] are necessary. This is how one learns what's happening in the cooperative. But then how do we know that they [the administration] are telling us the truth? They say, for example: 'we've spent seven million *soles* on this crop.' And how do we know? Maybe they spent only five, and put the rest in their pockets?" (field labourer)

Not surprisingly, all this led to a general lowering of interest in the assemblies, manifested in their diminishing frequency and in the decreasing requests from individual members. During the first two years after land reform (1973-4), thirty-six general assemblies were held. Twelve included a total of 115 individual requests. By contrast, during the twenty-two months from mid-1980 to mid-1982 the co-operative held only twenty-two assemblies, and only four raised individual requests, thirty-four in total.

Without effective worker participation in management, the co-operative's decisions became manipulated by the co-operative bureaucracy — the technical-administrative staff also controlling the Administrative Council. These manipulatory practices, however, were constantly challenged by an opposition group composed of some older labour union leaders and of younger, better educated workers or employees of worker origins. As a consequence of this challenge, the general assemblies in Siglo XX acquired a controversial, politicized character unlike the balanced, technical discussions at Alamos. The controversies, revolving mostly around the individual performance of members of the co-operative administration, reflected the workers' discontent with the skewed distribution of decisional power rooted in the co-operative occupational structure. This discontent manifested itself not only in the controversial general assemblies, but also in other, non-co-operative forms of internal organization. Unlike Alamos, the labour union in Siglo XX did not disappear after the co-operativization of the hacienda. It continued with the explicit objective of defending workers' interests and supervising the co-operative administration. In contrast to the co-operative institutions, the union represented manual workers almost exclusively, and its executive committee included more field labourers than the co-operative leadership. The union's meetings, uninhibited by the presence of the co-operative employees, had a more democratic, participatory character than co-operative assemblies. The union primarily negotiated with the co-operative administration over wage increases, disciplinary issues, and social programs. Occasionally, however, it also raised more general co-operative issues as, for example, in 1974, when it demanded an audit of co-operative accounts and a resignation of the Administrative Council dominated by the employees.

In addition to the co-operative union, one of the two remote field sectors (the one formed by local workers) retained its own labour union. This sectoral union not only obtained certain improvements in living conditions and transportation, but also offered its members classes in accounting to enable them to better control the co-operative administration. The other remote sector (formed by *serranos*) had no sectoral labour union, but was highly organized. All decisions in the sector were made by the sectoral assembly, which the field labourers considered much more responsive and effective in problem-solving than the co-operative meetings. The assembly elected ad hoc committees for dealing with particular work or communal problems. In 1980, for example, the *serrano* field labourers launched the so-called Defence Committee, which started by supervising the co-operative potato marketing and gradually attempted to monitor all factory transactions.

The co-operative members' involvement in organizational activities was, however, especially visible at the regional level. Contrary to Alamos, where members were overwhelmingly quite sceptical about the regional organizations, more than half of the respondents at Siglo XX (seven out of nine employees and eighteen out of forty-five rank-and-file workers) admitted that these organizations were engaged in some useful activities ranging from unspecified meetings and consultations to the provision of legal aid to co-operatives and the organization of strikes.

The co-operative's involvement in regional organizational activities dated back to the early 1970s. Immediately after land reform, the co-operative met with a refusal by the former owners to pay compensation (7.5 million *soles*, according to the co-operative's calculation) to the workers of the expropriated hacienda. Since a similar problem also existed in several other co-operatives of the valley, the Siglo XX union leadership organized an interco-operative Committee for Mutual Aid which presented the case to the local offices of the Ministry of Labour and the Agrarian Tribunal. These, however, were seeking a deal with the former owners rather than with the co-operatives.

Confronted with unresponsive local bureaucrats, the Committee took the case to Lima. The negotiations, in which the co-operatives were assisted by the General Confederation of Peruvian Workers (CGTP), lasted almost two years. By the end of this time, Siglo XX announced its decision to strike, publicizing it widely in the local and national press. Soon after, the case was solved in favour of the co-operatives. Most of the compensation was paid by the former owners through the Bank of the Nation; the rest was deducted by the co-operative from a short-term production loan extended by the Agrarian Bank.

In 1974, on the eve of the nationalization of cotton marketing, Siglo XX actively participated in the movement for the transfer of marketing to cotton producers (see Chapter 2). It sent delegates to a nation-wide meeting of cotton producers and held consultations with the government agencies involved. Later, one member served on the short-lived Commission for Cotton Marketing formed by state representatives and delegates from cotton co-operatives. Siglo XX also had a member serving on the CNA's Executive Committee and several others holding high-ranking positions in regional CNA-sponsored organizations. In 1979, when the regional Committee of Cotton Producers was organized, a member of Siglo XX became its first president. A year earlier, in 1978, another member was elected as the president of the regional Central Co-operative. Under his presidency, the Central Co-operative became involved in the direct marketing of food crops, an activity encouraged at that time by the CNA. Since local potato prices were relatively low, the Central Co-operative sent several truck loads of potatoes, mostly from Siglo XX's fields, directly to a retail market in Lima. This step aroused the protests of influential firms controlling local trade, and the experiment was promptly stopped. Nevertheless, Siglo XX continued to support CNA policies. When that same year, the government decided to withdraw official recognition from the CNA (see Chapter 3), it also tried to create an appearance of legitimacy for this measure by seeking support from local co-operative leaders. To the dismay of the CNA national leadership, most co-operative leaders in the valley agreed to sign the anti-CNA document prepared by government officials. The most notable exception was Siglo XX, whose leaders promptly printed and distributed flyers criticizing the government position and calling for solidarity with the CNA.

The CNA's influence at Siglo XX was reinforced by the predominance of leftist political orientations among its workers, which dated back to pre-reform times and contrasted sharply with the *aprista* tradition of many other co-operatives. As mentioned elsewhere, shortly before land reform, the hacienda union affiliated with the CGTP, which was influenced by the Communists. At the time of my field research, Siglo XX had the largest, most influential group of PSR members in the valley, most of whom had been recruited among the younger co-operative members, skilled labourers, and employees of working origins in particular.

Siglo XX's close relationship with regional and national political organizations was also manifested in its willingness to bring external actors into internal controversies, including the alleged cases of mismanagement and corruption. When the first financial scandal broke in 1974, the co-operative union's secretary general requested an audit of co-operative accounts under the supervision of SINAMOS. The request was ratified by the Assembly, but the co-operative administration was reluctant to implement the agreement. This led to a prolonged, bitter fight between the administration and the union's secretary general, supported by local SINAMOS officials. The involvement of SINAMOS in what many members considered a purely internal matter caused a certain degree of discontent in the co-operative. At one point, when SINAMOS requested some compromising financial documents from the co-operative, the relations between the two became strained. Caught between its habitual mistrust of the co-operative administration and its hostility toward the strangers, the Assembly still opted for a SINAMOS-sponsored audit. SINAMOS, and later the CNA, were called in by the co-operative labour union under similar circumstances on several other occasions.

MONTE BLANCO: BUREAUCRATIZATION WITHOUT POLITICIZATION

If Alamos had an effective system of worker participation in management and Siglo XX had an impressive record of intraco-operative and regional political struggles, Monte Blanco had neither. In terms of worker participation in co-operative management, Monte Blanco bore a certain similarity to Siglo XX. Of its ninety-three members, thirty-two (approximately one-third) had been members of the Administrative Council. Fifteen of these thirty-two had been reelected at least twice. Among these fifteen, six were employees; four, skilled labourers; and five, field labourers. In other words, employees and skilled workers dominated the elected co-operative leadership.

As at Siglo XX, the general assemblies had relatively little impact on actual co-operative management. "Who decides everything here? The manager. The manager and the president. They go back and forth, make contacts, buy and sell things. And people [workers] don't have the slightest idea of what's going on in the co-operative. Just get their pay on Saturday, and everybody — to drink!" (tractor driver).

Members' interest in the assemblies also tended to diminish. During the two years after land reform (1974-5), the co-operative held thirty-four assemblies, while during the two years preceding my field research, it held twenty-four. The number of assemblies including individual requests fell from twenty to thirteen, and the total number of requests fell from 237 to 184. Approximately half of all the requests (47 per cent in the first period and 53 per cent in the second period) came from the skilled labour force. Symptomatically, only three of the fourteen respondents believed that general assemblies were necessary in the co-operative (and among these three, two argued that they were good only for obtaining information or for discussion, but not for decisionmaking): "The assemblies, at least as we have them here, are completely useless. People don't have preparation to understand what is happening in the co-operative. They don't even listen to reports, just go on with their murmuring. All they can do is just murmur" (field labourer).

Unlike Siglo XX, the frustration with the co-operative institutions at Monte Blanco did not spark interest in unionist activities. Its tiny, relatively passive labour union disappeared soon after the co-operativization of the hacienda. In 1979, it was reorganized upon the Agrarian League's suggestion. This was, however, a sheer formality: since the reorganization not a single union assembly has been held. Clearly, Monte Blanco had failed to develop an internal worker opposition and complementary forms of organization, so prominent at Siglo XX. The members' evaluation of the activities of the regional organizations was also negative: all fourteen respondents agreed that the organizations did nothing for the co-operatives in the valley. In fact, Monte Blanco took part in some training programs for co-operative members. It also joined the Central Co-operative, the Agrarian League, and the Committee of Cotton Producers, dutifully paying its membership fees and sending delegates to their meetings and conferences. However, its members' attitude toward these organizations, and toward the Agrarian League in particular, was, on the whole, rather negative: "They make too much politics. I agree that we should try to defend co-operatives. All right, let's make a petition: prices, credit, interest rates, everything. But we should ask, negotiate, persuade. We should not act with arrogance; it means to turn the government against us. And those people [the League leadership] don't understand that. There are too many ambitions, too much party politics among them" (accountant). The PSR's attempt to gain ground in the co-operative largely failed. Generally speaking, Monte Blanco offered a remarkable resistance to all attempts by the Agrarian League or the CNA to influence its internal affairs. Its fear of external influences is illustrated by the following.

In 1979, a certain co-operative field labourer, C.H., committed serious infractions of the labour regulations. After several reprimands and warnings, the co-operative decided to expel him. C.H. appealed to the Agrarian League, alleging abuse by the co-operative administration. After a brief investigation, the League supported the appeal. It sent a letter to the co-operative, pointing out that both presidents of the co-operative councils, employees by occupation, had been closely associated with the former hacienda owners and that they had acted, in the case under consideration, with ill will. After the letter was read to the Assembly, this body lapsed into its usual anti-administration spirit and decided to "forgive" C.H. The events, however, took an unexpected turn when, as reported in the Book of Records, one co-operative employee asked:

"and who wrote the report to the Agrarian League for him?" [As everybody at Monte Blanco knew, C.H. was illiterate.] Member C.H. says that it was a certain lawyer from N. The Assembly unanimously decides that the Administrative Council should travel to N. and confirm this fact. Seeing this attitude, member C.H. confesses that actually it was not a lawyer from N., but member E.D. [a cooperative leader, employee by occupation, that was most closely involved with the League]. . . . The Assembly unanimously decides that member E.D. should be banned from the office and sent to work to the field as punishment for his attempts to initiate a conflict and to slander the co-operative before the Agrarian League. (Book of Records, 13 August 1979)

The field labourer involved did not save himself either. Several months later, he was expelled from the co-operative — not for his poor work performance, but for "slandering co-operative leaders before the Agrarian League" (Book of Records, 19 October 1979). Even his appeals to the Ministry of Agriculture did not help. Despite the Ministry's "recommendation" that C.H. continue working in the co-operative until his status was legally clarified, the Assembly insisted on his immediate expulsion.

It must be added that Monte Blanco had never permitted SINAMOS or the CNA to interfere in its financial affairs, which were even more complicated and obscure than those at Siglo xx. In 1975, the General Assembly at Monte Blanco requested an audit, but this was never carried out. In 1976, faced with another financial scandal, the Assembly asked for the co-operative councils to resign. After a protracted, confused debate, the council members got away with a "warning that in the future they should avoid committing similar errors" (Book of Records, 25 May 1976). In a similar vein, the 1981 and 1982 inventories of the co-operative warehouse uncovered serious irregularities. A commission of investigation was formed, but no definite conclusions were presented to the Assembly and no charged were ever laid.

Thus, both state-sponsored co-operatives, Siglo XX and Monte Blanco, failed to develop effective participation in management. They were too big and too complex in relation to their field labourers' ability to control the co-operative administration. As a consequence, the co-operative institutions came under the control of the co-operative bureaucracy composed of hacienda employees and co-opted worker-leaders. The bureaucratization of the co-operative institutions tended to reinforce the socio-economic differentiation among co-operative members, as discussed in Chapter 4. It also amplified and, in effect, institutionalized co-operative mismanagement and fuelled intraco-operative social conflicts. The workers' response was, however, quite different in both cases.

Siglo XX's membership, with its vast pre-reform organizational experience, produced more or less coherent and effective worker opposition to the co-operative bureaucracy. It also developed intraco-operative complementary organizations which, although not able to control the co-operative administration, at least challenged it constantly. Such worker opposition and complementary organizations were conspicuously absent at Monte Blanco, whose workers had very little organizational experience. The difference was further increased by the co-operatives' unequal involvement in regional/national politics. After co-operativization, Siglo XX led the regional co-operative movement, as it had led the trade union movement before it. In fact, Siglo XX turned into a PSR stronghold in the valley and developed close contacts with the Agrarian League and the CNA national leadership. By contrast, Monte Blanco had cautiously climbed on the bandwagon of the co-operative movement after land reform. Its willingness and ability to become involved in regional/national politics was insignificant, and its political contacts remained minimal.

CONCLUSION

The analysis of the co-operative institutions at Alamos, Siglo XX, and Monte Blanco seems to confirm the proposition about the bureaucratic nature of the state-sponsored co-operative movement, frequently made in the literature on Peru. The bureaucratic management characteristic of the state-sponsored Siglo XX and Monte Blanco contrasted sharply with the co-operative democracy practised by the independent Alamos. However, it should be noted that the bureaucratization of the co-operative institutions in both cases was caused not only by government officials' and hacienda employees' deliberate efforts to subordinate co-operative development to their national or private goals, but also, no less importantly, by the relatively low ability of most co-operative members to effectively control co-operative administration.

This fact could be largely explained by peculiarities of the organization of production on the pre-reform cotton haciendas. While Alamos was a relatively small estate with a predominantly stable, unionized, and largely literate labour force of local origin, Siglo XX was a big agroindustrial entreprise relying, to a large extent, on quasi-temporary, unorganized, and illiterate labourers, many recent migrants from the Sierra. The gap between the managerial complexity and the workers' organizational and educational experiences was also quite pronounced at Monte Blanco. Its membership was recruited primarily among unorganized quasi-temporary labourers and small tenants unfamiliar with centrally managed forms of production. As a consequence, the administration in both co-operatives became explicitly bureaucratic: the co-operative employees controlled the Administrative Council, and the Council manipulated the General Assembly.

The bureaucratization of co-operative institutions had obvious social and economic implications. It amplified socio-economic differentiation discussed in the previous chapter. It also institutionalized co-operative mismanagement which had seriously affected the economic performance of the state-sponsored co-operatives (see Chapter 6). The political implications of the rise of co-operative bureaucracy were, however, more complex. It would be wrong to assume that bureaucratization implied a gradual disappearance of all forms of worker participation in state-sponsored co-operatives. Nor did it always reduce this participation to the demands for short-term economic benefits only. The experience of Siglo XX indicates that co-operative bureaucracy could also raise an articulate opposition among the hacienda workers. At Siglo XX, this opposition was represented primarily by the co-operative labour unions and the Defence Committee. These organizations, composed almost exclusively of field labourers, did not limit themselves to defending workers' social and economic gains, but also challenged the co-operative relations of power, pressing for a more effective worker control of co-operative management. Worker opposition at Siglo XX was facilitated by its prereform trade union experiences, as well as by autonomous, non-cooperative forms of organization after land reform. Such opposition gave a distinctively political tone to Siglo XX's co-operative institutions, distinguishing it not only from the democratic management at Alamos, but also from the unchallenged rule of bureaucracy at Monte Blanco.

The co-operative institutions at Siglo XX were politicized from within and from without, as a consequence of the co-operative's close ties with the CNA. Siglo XX's involvement in regional and national politics contrasted sharply with the relative political passivity of both Alamos and Monte Blanco. This involvement continued Siglo XX's pre-reform trade union tradition transformed into co-operative militancy after land reform. The peculiar combination of trade union experience and participation in the state-sponsored co-operative movement produced a political activism unknown in the other two co-operatives.

The internal and external politicization modified the bureaucratic nature of the state-sponsored co-operative movement. It also influenced the co-operatives' responses to the economic crisis affecting the co-operative cotton economy in the early 1980s. Before analysing these responses, however, I shall examine the origins and the scope of the co-operatives' economic difficulties.

CHAPTER SIX

Co-Operative Economy in Crisis

The transition from populism to post-populism in Peru involved the gradual introduction of market-oriented policies, manifested in a general trend toward liberalization of domestic and foreign trade (see Chapter 3). In the cotton-growing sector, however, these policies affected mostly agricultural inputs (e.g., chemical fertilizers and pesticides). Cotton prices continued to be set by the government with an intention to subsidize the textile industry. Moreover, in the early 1980s, international cotton prices fell, causing a decline in domestic cotton prices already relatively low. The implications for co-operative cotton production were disastrous. In the second half of the 1970s and early 1980s, the increase in nominal and real cotton prices in the department selected for the case studies tended to lag behind the growth of cotton production costs (see Table 16).

The decline in the cotton co-operatives' sales revenues caused by these trends was aggravated by their dependence on short-term loans issued by the Agrarian Bank. As the Bank's interest rates rose (see Chapter 3), the co-operatives' financial dependence turned into indebtedness. As a consequence, some co-operatives in the valley were refused further credit, which drastically reduced their productive activities. Others had to mortgage their property to receive further financial assistance. When the field research was being carried out, no co-operative in the valley had yet been declared insolvent or lost its mortgaged property. However, the collapse of the co-operative system under the burden of debts was generally regarded as almost inevitable.

Alamos, Siglo xx, and Monte Blanco did not escape the negative effect of the post-populist economic policies. The scope of their eco-

TABLE 16: Evolving nominal and real cotton prices and production costs in Department, 1975-82*

	1975	1976	1977	1978	1979	1980	1981	1982
Nominal prices of cotton (*soles*/kg)	20.8	22.2	30.6	47.2	87.2	150.0	205.8	256.4
1975 = 100	(100)	(107)	(147)	(227)	(420)	(723)	(992)	(1,236)
Nominal costs of cotton production (1,000 *soles*/ha)	50.3	67.5	78.9	102.7	212.0	365.2	743.8	1,091.5
1975 = 100	(100)	(134)	(158)	(206)	(424)	(730)	(1,488)	(2,164)
Real prices of cotton (*soles*/kg)	11.5	9.1	8.8	8.3	15.0	9.7	8.4	7.6
1975 = 100	(100)	(78)	(71)	(72)	(131)	(84)	(73)	(66)
Real costs of cotton production (1,000 *soles*/ha)	30.0	28.5	22.4	16.3	20.6	23.5	29.4	31.1
1975 = 100	(100)	(95)	(75)	(54)	(68)	(79)	(98)	(103)

SOURCE: Statistical data from the Ministry of Agriculture, Departmental Office
*Real prices calculated in 1970 currency

TABLE 17: Structure of agricultural areas (%), Alamos, selected years

	73/74	74/75	76/77	80/81	81/82	82/83
Cotton	54	65	64	61	64	65
Grapes	—	—	15	24	25	27
Other crops	46	35	21	14	11	8
Total	100	100	100	100	100	100

SOURCE: Co-operative production plans

nomic difficulties, however, varied depending on the socio-economic and institutional make-up of each of the three co-operatives.

ALAMOS. AN EFFICIENT ECONOMY UNDER STRAIN

After land reform, Alamos, like most other co-operatives in the valley, continued to specialize in cotton growing. Cotton accounted for almost two-thirds of its total sales, followed by grapes (see Table 17). The decision to introduce grapes was made after the co-operativization of the hacienda, in view of the deteriorating prospects

TABLE 18: Indicators of co-operative economic performance at Alamos, 1975-82*

	1975	1976	1977	1978	1979	1980	1981	1982
Sales	43.2	36.4	46.4	98.8	207.1	360.4	522.6	664.3
1975 = 100	(100)	(84)	(107)	(229)	(479)	(834)	(1,210)	(1,538)
Costs	32.7	32.4	33.9	73.4	111.9	188.9	307.6	450.0
1975 = 100	(100)	(99)	(104)	(224)	(342)	(577)	(941)	(1,367)
Financial expenses	0.8	—	3.5	3.8	8.6	9.1	74.1	185.8
1975 = 100	(100)	—	(438)	(475)	(1,075)	(1,138)	(9,263)	(23,225)
Administrative expenses	5.5	6.3	9.8	15.4	32.7	77.9	166.9	280.9
1975 = 100	(100)	(114)	(178)	(280)	(595)	(1,416)	(3,035)	(5,109)
Revenues	10.5	4.0	12.5	25.4	95.2	171.5	215.0	214.3
Earnings	2.1	4.2	3.3	13.7	62.6	95.6	49.1	-65.6
Profits	1.4	3.5	1.6	2.8	22.1	16.2	0	-65.6
Short-term debt (principal as of June 30)	5.3	9.1	9.8	3.1	0.0	0.0	24.3	298.0

SOURCE: Co-operative income statements and balance sheets
   *All indicators calculated in 1,000 current *soles* per ha of irrigated land

for irrigation. The co-operative also started growing two other perennial crops, oranges and pecans, but on a very small scale.[1]

The impact of the economic crisis on co-operative performance at Alamos was relatively mild. Alamos was *the* most profitable co-operative in the valley. Contrary to the regional and national trends in the cotton-growing sector, production costs at Alamos grew more slowly than the value of sales (see Table 18).

Comparing Alamos' indexes of growth with the departmental ones (keeping in mind, of course, that the latter refer exclusively to the cotton economy) shows that what distinguished Alamos from most other cotton producers was an extraordinarily low increase in production costs. Moreover, the Alamos' costs were considerably below the average cotton production costs in the department throughout the period in question (compare Tables 16 and 18). This phenomenon does not lend itself to an easy technical explanation. In terms of the use of agricultural machinery, fertilizers, and pesticides, Alamos did not differ considerably from other co-operatives in the valley (see Appendix 3). Further, Alamos had a certain disadvantage with regard to irrigation costs: it had no access to the local river (as, for example, Monte Blanco did), and therefore all the required water had to be pumped. In addition, Alamos' wells were equipped with oil and not

TABLE 19: Outlays for remuneration of permanent labour force per ha of irrigated lands, Alamos, selected years

	1975		1978		1979	
	per 1,000 soles	%	per 1,000 soles	%	per 1,000 soles	%
Stable labour force	1.6	99	21.1	100	100	100
Quasi-temporary labour force	0.1	1	—	—	—	—
Total	1.7	100	21.1	100	100	100

SOURCE: Co-operative payroll accounts

electrical pumps (as they were, for example, at Siglo XX). This pushed up Alamos' irrigation costs even further.[2] As for the co-operative labour force, Alamos did not have any obvious advantage either. By 1978 all the co-operative's tasks, apart from cotton picking, were being performed by co-operative members whose wages were considerably higher than those of quasi-temporary labourers (see Table 19).

Thus, the low production costs at Alamos should probably be attributed to the relatively low co-operative wages combined with a highly satisfactory work performance among manual labourers and an efficient management (see Chapters 4 and 5). These factors, in turn, could be largely explained by the drastic reduction in the hacienda occupational differences (which relieved the pressure for higher wages among field labourers) and by the effective operation of the co-operative administrative institutions. The co-operative's traditions of thrift and self-reliance, reflecting its independent origins, also played an important role.

Alamos' success in keeping down its production costs accounts for the fact that, even after the crisis began, it was able to sell its agricultural output at a profit. Its revenues from sales, however, were wiped out by skyrocketing administrative expenses. In the co-operative accounts, this term referred not only to administrative costs as such, but also to the so-called financial expenses, which include, most importantly, bank interest charges. While in 1975, the financial expenses of Alamos constituted 13 per cent of total administrative expenses, in 1982, their share rose to 66 per cent. At the same time, their amount per hectare grew much faster than either the co-operative's sales or even the production costs. The exorbitant growth of financial expenses reflected both the growth of production costs and the increase in interest rates, as well as the sluggish performance of the chronically underfinanced ENCI, the state-owned cotton marketing company. In the 1980s, Alamos used to receive the total payment for its cotton sales several months after the actual date of the transaction, which, of course, increased even further the interest it paid to the Agrarian Bank (the same was true for most other co-operatives in the valley). As a consequence, in 1980, the co-operative's net earnings left after the deduction of administrative expenses from the revenues from sales fell much more abruptly than the revenues themselves (see Table 18).

Alamos used part of its net earnings for cancelling annual payments for the purchased land and, from 1977 on, for paying co-operative income tax. The profits remaining after all these deductions were used for co-operative needs, including reinvestment. In 1977, co-operatives were also entitled to use up to 20 per cent of their net earnings for reinvestment, which Alamos did to finance its electrification project. The project was designed to switch the co-operative's irrigation system from oil to electrical energy to reduce production costs. It was financed partly by the co-operative itself and partly by the Inter-American Development Bank (through the Agrarian Bank). In 1981, however, the electrification works had to be postponed because of the co-operative's financial difficulties. As a result, Alamos was left without electrical pumps, but with considerable long-term debts (in 1982, 50 million *soles*, principal).

The dependence on the Agrarian Bank when interest rates kept increasing (even if they increased slower than inflation rates) was viewed by most co-operative members as a major cause of the co-operative financial crisis. In 1979, Alamos attempted to create its own operating capital. Since the co-operative gained good revenues that year, all members received substantial overtime pay which they returned to the co-operative as their contributions to the new operating capital fund. The co-operative paid interest on these contributions, although at a much lower rate than the rates charged by the Agrarian Bank. The fund reached 5.8 million *soles*, which, in 1980, allowed Alamos to cover approximately 20 per cent of the total production costs. In 1981, however, the extra-payments and, accordingly, the members' contributions, had to be slashed. In 1982, the co-operative's operating capital still remained the same as in 1979 — 6 million *soles* — while production costs over the same period more than doubled.

In sum, faced with the financial crisis, Alamos had to abandon its plans for switching to electrical energy and diminishing its dependence on the state credit system. Worse yet, it found itself unable to repay its loans to the Agrarian Bank (see Table 18). I must emphasize, however, that co-operative indebtedness was a recent phenomenon at Alamos directly related to the economic crisis of the 1980s.

The importance of external factors in the co-operative's economic crisis was reflected in its members' views on the origin of the crisis. In interviews, respondents were asked to indicate whether, in their opinion, the current economic difficulties were caused primarily by external factors (government price and credit policies) or by co-operative internal problems (the lack of labour discipline and mismanagement).

Almost all respondents at Alamos (seventeen out of nineteen) argued that the co-operative's difficulties were largely caused by government economic policies.

"This is a bad year because the production costs have increased too much. Oil is extremely expensive now. Fertilizers, pesticides, herbicides — everything is expensive. And the price of cotton doesn't rise. It has been the same for two years — 38 thousand [soles]. Do you think that with all that a co-operative may be in good shape? And on top of it, ENCI doesn't pay for the cotton on time. It's always late, sometimes more than two months. The payments come late, but we have to pay interest charges all the same. And the interest rate is now 55 per cent! As it is, we are just working for the bank." (field labourer)

The same story was repeated, with slight variations, by the other sixteen respondents, members of the co-operative administration (elected leaders, for the most part) and rank-and-file workers alike. Some respondents, skilled labourers in particular, also pointed to a certain deterioration in labour discipline. Nobody, however, mentioned corruption or mismanagement. Moreover, many informants proudly attributed the economic viability of their co-operative to strong internal solidarity and efficient worker control of the administration.

"This co-operative is better off than others. Here we are all members, there are no engineer-agronomists. Everything is ours, so that people work with endeavour. Besides, there is more control here, more respect [for co-operative property]. All administrative positions are elected. The only difference between, let's say, me and the president is that this year he happens to be president and I don't. As for the rest of it, we are equal. And we all know each other, we know each other's weaknesses or problems. It's like in a family. So that there can be hardly any irregularities, as you will find in other co-operatives. (field labourer)

I turn now to the economic situation of the other two co-operatives.

SIGLO XX: ON THE BRINK OF BANKRUPTCY

Like Alamos, Siglo XX was a cotton-growing co-operative, with part of

TABLE 20: Structure of agricultural areas (%), Siglo XX, selected years

	72/73	74/75	80/81	81/82	83/84
Cotton	60	71	73	80	81
Potatoes	12	10	13	11	11
Others	28	19	14	9	8
Total	100	100	100	100	100

SOURCE: Co-operative production plans

its lands growing potatoes and minor food and industrial crops (see Table 20).

The choice of potatoes as the second crop was determined by their generally high profitability and by the co-operative's extensive modern irrigation system. In good years, such as 1980 or 1982, potato sales brought Siglo XX good revenues (in 1982 almost equal to cotton revenues). In 1981, however, low potato prices added to the cotton crisis.

The economic crisis affected Siglo XX much more than Alamos. In the mid-1970s its sales per hectare were considerably higher than those of Alamos, which might have been due to the better quality of its cotton fibre, since the yields in both co-operatives were approximately the same. However, during the period in question, sales at Siglo XX grew at a lower rate. As for production costs at Siglo XX, not only were they much higher over the entire period under consideration, but also they grew much faster than at Alamos. Reflecting the general departmental trend, the rate of growth of the production costs at Siglo XX persistently outpaced the rate in the growth of sales; finally, in 1981 the co-operative's costs exceeded its sales (see Table 21).

A rigorous analysis of the origins of this situation lies beyond the scope of this book. Nevertheless, it must be noted that Siglo XX and Alamos made similar use of agricultural machinery, fertilizers, and pesticides (for cotton, see Appendix 3). Moreover, Siglo XX had a certain advantage in terms of its irrigation infrastructure: since 1976 almost all of its wells had been powered by electrical energy.[3]

As for the structure of the co-operative labour force, Siglo XX, unlike Alamos, continued to use cheap quasi-temporary labour (see Table 22). Despite this, the total outlay for remuneration of the permanent labour force (including the stable and the quasi-temporary labourers) in relation to the agricultural area, was 50 per cent higher at Siglo XX than at Alamos.

Given these considerations, it seems plausible to suggest that the high production costs at Siglo XX were primarily related to the co-operative's socio-economic and institutional peculiarities, as dis-

TABLE 21: Indicators of co-operative economic performance at Siglo XX, 1975-82*

	1975	1976	1977	1978	1979	1980	1981	1982
Sales	59.0	61.0	108.9	320.1	488.5	—	566.8	—
1975 = 100	(100)	(104)	(185)	(307)	(543)	(828)	(961)	—
Costs	38.3	41.2	73.7	120.4	201.4	325.4	597.6	—
1975 = 100	(100)	(107)	(192)	(314)	(526)	(850)	(1,560)	—
Financial expenses	3.0	3.8	—	9.7	29.5	42.2	140.7	—
1975 = 100	(100)	(126)	—	(323)	(983)	(1,407)	(4,690)	—
Administrative expenses	15.2	9.4	—	30.9	72.0	145.4	221.5	—
1975 = 100	(100)	(62)	—	(203)	(474)	(957)	(1,457)	—
Revenues	20.7	19.9	35.2	60.5	118.7	163.1	-30.8	—
Earnings	5.6	8.0	21.0	28.3	37.3	5.2	-246.3	—
Profits	2.4	2.0	3.7	7.8	9.2	0	-246.3	—
Short-term debt (principal as of 31 Dec.)	16.5	28.2	30.6	56.9	84.3	198.8	421.1	—

SOURCE: Co-operative income statements and balance sheets
*All indicators calculated in 1,000 current *soles* per hectare of irrigated land

cussed in the previous chapters. The growth of the hacienda stable labour force after land reform combined with the expansive promotional policies and generous wage increases pushed up the co-operative's production costs. The costs were further increased by the deterioration of labour discipline among manual labourers, manifested in the co-operative's continuing reliance on quasi-temporary labour. Furthermore, the high costs reflected the co-operative mismanagement caused by corruption among employees and aggravated by the bureaucratization of co-operative institutions.

The high production costs, in turn, increased Siglo XX's reliance on short-term credit and boosted its financial expenses. During the period under consideration, these expenses doubled and then tripled the financial expenses of Alamos. The administrative expenses also grew because of the ambitious social programs carried out by Siglo XX before the crisis began (see Table 21). Curiously, financial expenses at Siglo XX grew slower than they did in Alamos, probably because Siglo XX repeatedly deferred paying its interest charges to the Agrarian Bank. Still, this growth reinforced the negative effect of the increase in production costs: the co-operative net earnings fell in 1980 and turned into losses in 1981. Profits disappeared in 1980.[4]

TABLE 22: Outlays for remuneration of permanent labour force per ha of irrigated land, Siglo XX, selected years

	1975		1978		1979	
	per 1,000 soles	%	per 1,000 soles	%	per 1,000 soles	%
Stable labour force	10.1	71	25.4	83	136.9	89
Quasi-temporary labour force	4.1	29	5.2	17	16.6	11
Total	14.2	100	30.6	100	153.5	100

SOURCE: Co-operative payroll accounts

Ironically, in the mid-1970s, Siglo XX was much more profitable than Alamos: its net earnings and profits per hectare far exceeded those obtained by Alamos. However, Siglo XX's economic situation had already started to show signs of deterioration in 1979 (still a very good year for Alamos), and in the two subsequent years it experienced a much more dramatic decline than was the case at Alamos.

Another striking peculiarity of Siglo XX as compared with Alamos was its profound indebtedness to the Agrarian Bank (see Table 21). Actual figures on their debts cannot be legitimately compared because they refer to different periods (the budget year ends on 30 June at Alamos and 31 December at Siglo XX). However, by comparing the trends in indebtedness, it is clear that, unlike Alamos, the short-term debt at Siglo XX kept growing along with production costs and administrative expenses, even before the crisis. By 1981, the co-operative's short-term debt to the Agrarian Bank had reached an astronomical 778,641 million *soles* (principal). In 1982, Siglo XX had to mortgage its cotton gin to obtain credit for the forthcoming growing season.

The short-term debt to the Agrarian Bank formed only part of the co-operatives' current liabilities, which also included interest charges due to the Agrarian Bank, minor debts to private banks, and deferred social insurance and income tax payments. Once again, an accurate comparison of the current liabilities at Alamos and Siglo XX is impossible because of their different budget years. However, a simple glance at these figures, and especially their comparison with the co-operatives' assets, reveals the difference in their indebtedness. On 30 June 1981, the current liabilities at Alamos amounted to 32 million *soles*, which constituted less than half of the co-operative's current assets (including the inventory). The current liabilities at Siglo XX, on 31 December 1981, reached 1,223 million, exceeding the co-operative's current assets (1,022 million, the inventory included) and getting dangerously close to its total assets (1,229 million). How did Siglo XX's members view the causes of this financial disaster?

Most respondents (thirty-three out of fifty-four) believed that the co-operative crisis had been primarily caused by internal problems and not by government policies. The proportion of such internally oriented respondents was slightly lower among the interviewed members of the co-operative administration (all co-operative employees). Five argued that the crisis was the responsibility of the government, while the other four emphasized the importance of internal factors: poor work performance and redundancy. The social background of the externally and the internally oriented employees is remarkably different. Four of the five employees who blamed the government were younger office clerks with some secondary or university education promoted to their positions after land reform. The fifth was an overseer, also promoted after the co-operative was formed. While sharing the younger clerks' views, he also pointed to the deterioration in labour discipline. As for the four internally oriented employees, three were more than fifty years old and had held their positions since pre-reform times. Two were overseers with some primary education, and one was an office clerk with an incomplete secondary education.

The relationship between the informants' background and their position toward the crisis could also be seen in the case of manual workers. Among the workers who singled out economic policies as the major source of the crisis, two social categories were somewhat overrepresented: first, the skilled workers; and second, the field labourers who had served on the Administrative Council or who had held some other, less important, administrative positions.

Most externally oriented workers at Siglo XX developed the same argument as their counterparts at Alamos, making references to high interest rates, low agricultural prices, and so on. Some, however, displayed an amazing awareness of the broader political changes taking place in the country.

"At the beginning, it was all right. The government of Phase One [1968-75] used to give us all sorts of facilities. They gave us good cotton prices, they lent us as much money as we needed at a low interest rate. The problems started with the government of Phase Two [1975-1980]. And when Belaunde came to power, it became even worse than before. This gentleman wants co-operatives to go bankrupt, so that he could give the land back to *patrones*. That's why he keeps prices of our crops low, while the costs of production grow every day. And that's why he buys things abroad. A government should not buy food abroad. It's like in a family where the father doesn't tell his children what he wants them to sow, and then goes to buy crops from his nephews." (field labourer)

Moreover, some externally oriented workers took pains to enlighten their fellows about the external origins of the crisis.

"The costs of production have grown too much. . . . And the prices of our crops don't rise. . . . That's why we have losses. But people don't understand that. Some say field workers don't work well. Others say they steal at the factory. People don't know and they don't want to know. One works all day in the field, comes home, eats, sleeps — and that's all. How many times I've been fighting with my own wife, with fellows over here. Look, I used to tell them. I'll give you an example. If you buy a cow for fifty thousand [soles] and sell it for forty, are you going to make a profit? But people just go on with their "this one is stealing and that one is stealing . . . ." (field labourer)

As the informant himself admitted, explaining the co-operative's financial difficulties by reference to external factors had not been entirely successful. Most workers probably agreed that buying a cow for fifty thousand and selling it for forty was not good business, but they were inclined to blame the owners of the cow for the bad deal. Twenty-three of the thirty-three interviewed field labourers and six out of eleven skilled workers believed that the main source of the crisis lay inside, not outside, the co-operative. And all agreed that the main responsibility for this rested on the co-operative administration.

MONTE BLANCO: ON THE BRINK OF BANKRUPTCY

I shall turn now to the economic performance of the last co-operative studied, Monte Blanco. Like the two other co-operatives, Monte Blanco was mostly engaged in the cultivation of cotton, followed in importance by industrial cereals serving as inputs for the food processing industry: wheat, sorghum, and barley (see Table 23).

TABLE 23: Structure of agricultural areas (%), Monte Blanco, selected years

	74/75	76/77	77/78	78/79	79/80	80/81	81/82
Cotton	83	76	71	67	68	71	73
Cereals	—	20	13	14	13	12	20
Others	17	4	16	19	19	17	7
Total	100	100	100	100	100	100	100

SOURCE: Co-operative production plans

The co-operative also cultivated potatoes and grapes, but on a very small scale. Generally speaking, the diversity of crops at Monte Blanco was higher than it was at the two other co-operatives, even though many minor crops at Monte Blanco were persistently sold at a loss.

The 1980 crisis at Monte Blanco was comparable to that at Siglo XX and far exceeded that at Alamos. This was particularly significant because Monte Blanco, compared to Alamos, had at least two important advantages with regard to the structure of production costs. First, approximately one-third of all Monte Blanco's irrigation needs were satisfied by the water supply from the local river — an enviable situation given the rapidly increasing energy prices. Second, like Siglo XX, Monte Blanco continued to employ cheap quasi-temporary labour. In 1980, this category accounted for approximately one-fourth of its outlays for the remuneration of the permanent labour force (including the stable and the quasi-temporary labourers). These relative advantages did not prevent a rapid growth in production costs at Monte Blanco. Actually, its costs grew even faster than those of Siglo XX. Whereas in 1975, production costs at Monte Blanco were lower than at Alamos, in the 1980s they approached Siglo XX's. Moreover, as at Siglo XX, the growth in costs outpaced the increase in co-operative sales, until finally, in 1980, they reached approximately the same level (see Table 24).

TABLE 24: Indicators of co-operative economic performance at Monte Blanco, 1975-82*

	1975	1976	1977	1978	1979	1980	1981	1982
Sales	33.1	—	74.0	120.1	231.2	333.7	412.1	736.0
1975 = 100	(100)	—	(224)	(363)	(698)	(1,008)	(1,245)	(2.224)
Costs	23.0	—	54.7	94.8	162.2	220.7	485.4	696.9
Financial expenses	—	—	3.2	4.7	19.8	63.0	159.0	318.5
Administrative expenses	6.7	—	13.6	16.4	39.0	109.7	215.5	410.8
1975 = 100	(100)	—	(202)	(245)	(582)	(1,637)	(3,216)	(6,131)
Revenues	10.1	—	19.3	25.3	69.0	0.1	-73.3	39.1
Earnings	3.9	—	5.4	9.7	32.1	6.4	-276.0	-382.0
Profits	2.0	—	1.7	2.8	8.3	0	-276.0	-382.0
Short-term debt (principal as of 31 Dec.)	19.5	—	31.5	41.2	82.8	178.4	430.5	703.5

SOURCE: Co-operative income statements and balance sheets
*All indicators calculated in 1,000 current *soles* per hectare of irrigated land

The exorbitant growth of production costs at Monte Blanco seemed to be largely due to the same socio-economic and institutional factors which had pushed up production costs at Siglo XX. Even though the membership and promotion policies at Monte Blanco were more restrictive than they were at Siglo XX, the generous increases to the stable field labourers led to the rapid growth in the co-operative's outlays for remuneration. This growth was also due to the relaxation of labour discipline in the field (aggravated at Monte Blanco by the preservation of private agriculture within the co-operative bounda-ries). Finally, the corruption among employees and the deficient oper-ation of the co-operative institutions were also important factors. In effect, at Monte Blanco they could have been even more important in precipitating the co-operative crisis than at Siglo XX, whose workers were somewhat more involved — albeit in a sporadic, controversial fashion — in co-operative management.

The rapid increase in the co-operative's production costs was paral-leled by growing financial and administrative expenses (see Table 24). This growth was particularly dramatic for financial expenses, whose proportion in the total administrative expenditures increased from 24 per cent in 1977 to 78 per cent in 1982. In 1977, the financial expenses per hectare at Monte Blanco were approximately the same as at Ala-mos; in the 1980s, they exceeded not only the expenses of Alamos, but also those of Siglo XX — probably because, unlike Siglo XX, Monte Blanco did not defer its interest charges.[5]

The rapid growth of production costs and administrative expenses at Monte Blanco accounted for huge losses in the early 1980s, losses comparable to those of Siglo XX. As for the trends of indebtedness, Monte Blanco was also quite similar to Siglo XX: its short-term debt to the Agrarian Bank was growing steadily over the period in question, along with production costs and administrative expenses (see Table 24). Actually, Monte Blanco's financial situation on 31 December 1981 was almost identical to that of Siglo XX. Its current liabilities amounted to 347 million *soles*, of which 336 million were in short-term debts to the Agrarian Bank (principal).

Even more than at Siglo XX, the co-operative members at Monte Blanco were inclined to ascribe the origin of this catastrophe to the misfunctioning of co-operative institutions. With one exception, all respondents argued that the recent deterioration in the co-operative economy was caused by internal problems. Nine out of fourteen respondents at Monte Blanco were manual workers, and all nine blamed the crisis on the co-operative administration: "It's because in this co-operative there is no respect for anything. Look, suppose a genteleman takes the president's office for a year. And here we go:

he's already got a car, a color TV. Where did he get the money? Ah? You don't know? All right. Let's say you are the president, and this lady here is the manager. You are going to steal with her, aren't you? Do you see now?" (field labourer).

By contrast, four of the five interviewed employees argued that the crisis was caused by the field labourers' poor work performance. Only one mentioned government policies as the main source of the co-operative's economic difficulties.

CONCLUSION

The analysis of the co-operatives' economic performance indicates that post-populist economic policies, discussed in Chapter 3, had a disastrous effect on the cotton co-operatives. In the early 1980s, all three co-operatives studied experienced serious economic difficulties. To a large extent, these difficulties were related to the jump in the prices of agricultural inputs and in bank interest rates, combined with relatively low cotton prices. These negative external factors affected all three but to different degrees. The co-operatives' vulnerability to the economic crisis depended, to a large extent, on their ability to hold back production costs. In this connection, a distinction can be made between two styles of co-operative performance: "conservative" at Alamos and "expansive" at Siglo XX and Monte Blanco.

Co-operative sales and, especially, production costs at Alamos grew much slower than in the two other co-operatives; Alamos' attitude toward bank credit and administrative spending was also much more cautious. In the 1970s, while inflation and interest rates were still relatively low, the difference in economic outcomes was not very noticeable: Alamos made more profits than Monte Blanco, but less than Siglo XX. However, in the early 1980s, Alamos' ability to curb its spending became an invaluable asset, which enabled it to obtain revenues from sales when the other two had already failed to do so. This ability also allowed Alamos to keep its losses and debts at moderate levels.

The difference in styles was largely related to the co-operatives' origins and relations with the state. Independent Alamos took pains to achieve financial self-reliance, while state-sponsored Siglo XX and Monte Blanco indulged in massive borrowing from the Agrarian Bank. The financial support, obtained easily at the earlier stages of their existence, induced the state-sponsored co-operatives to improve the economic and social position of their permanent labour force in a way undreamed of at Alamos. As demonstrated in Chapters 4 and 5, Siglo XX and Monte Blanco extended co-operative membership to their numerous quasi-temporary labourers, thereby swelling their stable labour force. They also granted generous wage increases to their workers and carried out ambitious social programs. The scope of these improvements, as compared to the situation at Alamos, indicates that the state-sponsored co-operatives enjoyed considerable success in using their dependence on the state to the advantage of the rural labour force. Of course, this success depended on the government's willingness to support the co-operative sector, a willingness that declined progressively after the fall of the Velasco government. Moreover, the success was offset by the policy of agricultural price controls, the increase in interest rates, and by the introduction of co-operative income tax. Nevertheless, state financial support enabled the state-sponsored co-operatives to grant substantial economic and social benefits to their labour force, benefits which inflated their production costs and increased their vulnerability to changes in the national economic conjuncture.

The rapid growth of spending in the state-sponsored co-operatives reflected their reliance on state credit and their internal socio-economic and institutional peculiarities, as discussed earlier. At Siglo XX and Monte Blanco, socio-economic differentiation through private economic activities was accompanied by deteriorating labour discipline among field labourers and corruption among employees. The bureaucratization of co-operative institutions augmented the scope of these phenomena and reinforced co-operative mismanagement. These problems — absent at Alamos, with its high levels of social equality and co-operative democracy — contributed to mounting production costs and administrative expenses at Siglo XX and Monte Blanco.

The differences in co-operative performance were reflected in the members' views on the co-operative economic crisis. Nobody at Alamos had any doubt about the external origin of their economic difficulties. By contrast, in the two state-sponsored co-operatives, most members believed that these difficulties were caused by mismanagement and poor labour discipline. However, the proportion of these internally oriented members was considerably lower at Siglo XX. Approximately one-third of the respondents in this co-operative were inclined to attribute the origin of the crisis to government economic policies. Such externally oriented members were almost absent at Monte Blanco.

As I shall show in Chapter 7, the members' views on the causes of co-operative difficulties had influenced their responses to the economic crisis, which varied considerably from co-operative to co-operative.

CHAPTER SEVEN

Co-Operative Responses to the Economic Crisis

The co-operative economic crisis set in motion apparently contradictory events. It reactivated the co-operative movement, discussed with reference to national development in Chapter 3. In the valley selected for the case studies, the post-reform co-operative sector was represented most importantly by two organizations: the Agrarian League affiliated with the CNA and composed of twenty cotton production co-operatives, and the regional Committee of Cotton Producers (a member of the national Committee of Cotton Producers) formed by the same twenty co-operatives, plus approximately two hundred small and medium individual producers (owning between 5 and 50 ha of irrigated land each). Confronted with the co-operative crisis, these organizations created a regional Front for the Defence of Agriculture which, however, failed to develop into one of the broad, militant coalitions dominating regional politics in other areas of the country. As for the League and the Committee as such, they became effectively involved in various political activities, especially the co-operative mobilization against land devolutions and government agricultural policies.

The devolutions of expropriated estates to their former owners reflected the beginning of the neo-liberal counter-reform (see Chapter 3). In 1981, the regional Land Court ordered a devolution of one expropriated estate to the former owner, claiming abandonment by the co-operative. A year later, the regional branch of the Ministry of Agriculture reversed the 1975 resolution on the expropriation of still another local estate, which had also been transformed into co-operative property. The co-operatives in question, assisted by the

Agrarian League, not only appealed the above decisions in court, but also "took over" the disputed estates, barricading their entrances. The takeovers were supported by most other co-operatives in the valley, and proved to be quite effective: in both cases, the co-operatives succeeded, at least temporarily, in retaining the disputed land. The mobilization in defence of co-operative land culminated in two strikes called in August and November 1982 by the CNA, together with other national agrarian organizations, to protest government agricultural policies — price and credit policies in particular (see Chapter 3). Both the League and the Committee joined the strikes, although private producers (members of the Committee) preferred to ignore the decision of their leadership. As for the co-operatives, on both occasions they blocked the PanAmerican Highway, interrupting traffic and successfully resisting police attempts to dismantle the barricades.

These political events demonstrated that in the crisis of the early 1980s the co-operatives of the valley exerted considerable political pressure in defence of the co-operative sector. This pressure, however, was not the only response to their economic difficulties. As argued in Chapter 6, the co-operative crisis reflected the post-populist change in national economic policies and the co-operatives' internal problems. As such, it also called for internal solutions to reduce their swollen production costs. One solution was a reorganization of the co-operatives' labour and administration relations. Ironically, the most noticeable attempt at such a reorganization involved not a rationalization of the sluggish co-operative production, but a change in the co-operatives' relations with the temporary labour force.

The relations between temporary labourers (cotton pickers for the most part) and co-operative members had always been strained. Friction dated back to pre-reform times when the organized stable labourers obtained considerable concessions from the hacienda management, while the unorganized temporary labourers were employed without contracts for starvation wages. Friction persisted after land reform which benefitted the stable labourers (transforming them into co-operative members), but which did not do much to improve the situation of the temporary labourers. Only a few were granted co-operative membership along with the stable labourers. Co-operatives, however, started to issue written contracts to their temporary labourers, granting them access in this way to fringe benefits such as health insurance, holiday pay, and social bonuses. These modest improvements were wiped out in the early 1980s. Confronted with the economic crisis, co-operatives reduced their expenses to curb production costs. Since co-operative members did not favour internal cutbacks, the easiest way to cut costs was by slashing expenses on temporary labour. Co-operatives could do this either by substituting co-operative members for temporary labourers during the harvest or by doing away with written contracts. Given the co-operative members' reluctance to pick cotton, most co-operatives in the valley opted for the second alternative, returning to the pre-reform practice of *enganche*, whereby temporary labourers, both seasonal migrants and local residents, were brought to a hacienda by a private contractor who paid them wages without fringe benefits. As could be expected, this measure soured relations between co-operatives and temporary workers, so much so that some of their leaders started talking about invading co-operative lands, actions which could certainly create the appearance of popular support for land devolutions.

The co-operatives' attempts to reduce their production costs by reorganizing labour relations implied the preservation of production co-operatives created by land reform. As such, these attempts were compatible with the first type of response to the crisis — political mobilization. However, in some cases, the search for internal solutions took a different course. Faced with the rapid deterioration of their economy, some co-operatives turned to the subdivision of their lands, presumably, as a way out of the crisis. In contrast to reorganization, subdivision involved a dissolution of production co-operatives and a transition to small-scale agriculture. If implemented on a large scale, it would have resulted in the disintegration of the post-reform co-operative movement, at least in its present form. Subdivision, however, was still quite new in the valley. In 1983, at the time of the field research, only two out of twenty local production co-operatives had actually subdivided their lands. Below, I examine various co-operative responses to the crisis, focusing on the position of each co-operative toward political mobilization, reorganization, and subdivision.

ALAMOS: ''WAIT AND SEE''

Since Alamos had been less affected by the crisis than the other two co-operatives, its search for solutions was less urgent than Siglo xx's or Monte Blanco's. Alamos joined the regional co-operative mobilization but, apprehensive about its political implications, did so without much enthusiasm.

"Take this case of H. [the co-operative which had its land disputed by the former owner]. Of course, I don't agree with it [with the owner's claims]. Land should belong to those who work it. But this is also a political game: it's political parties who pick on it right away. Here, for example, they came to talk about China. Why China? What on earth has it to do with our troubles? I have never liked political parties, and here we don't permit them to meddle with the co-operative. At home, you can do whatever you want, but in the co-operative — no way." (well operator)

Another factor which accounted for Alamos' reserve about collective action was a widespread belief by members that other co-operatives in the valley were in a crisis because of mismanagement and poor work performance, so that land devolution in their case appeared inevitable, even legitimate.

"Look what happened in S.C. [the co-operative which sold one of its estates to its former owner]. That estate had been abandoned because they had neither water nor money to work it. That's exactly how *patrones* are going to come back — grabbing lands which co-operatives cannot work. And some people in co-operatives are so desperate now that they start saying: 'That's all right, let them come back!' The *patrones* always had money [to work the land], they are all millionaires!" (field labourer)

Finally, because Alamos purchased its land directly from private owners while other co-operatives received theirs through land reform, its members were relatively secure in their land rights.

If Alamos' attitude toward political mobilization was rather lukewarm, it was not very keen on internal reorganization either. The possibilities of reducing co-operative expenses were rather limited since Alamos already had extraordinarily low production costs and relatively few social services. Alamos' only step in this direction was the suspension of interest-free credit for its members. Significantly, Alamos was the only co-operative in the valley that did not try to solve its financial problems at the expense of the temporary labourers. During the 1982 harvest season, Alamos continued to issue written contracts to cotton pickers, as it had done before the crisis began. To a certain extent, this could be explained by the relative mildness of the crisis at Alamos. However, the nature of its relations with the temporary labourers had also imposed certain constraints on its freedom of action. In contrast to most other co-operatives, Alamos' cotton pickers were not seasonal migrants, but primarily local residents who had come to the valley from the Sierra in the 1960s and who had settled down in the same village where the stable hacienda labourers lived. The shared residential experience made Alamos' members more responsive to the temporary labourers' needs. In addition, the temporary labourers organized their own Association of Landless Peasants (the only successful one in the valley), which effectively used pressure in negotiating with the co-operative administration. In 1981, for instance, its members went on strike in mid-harvesting, obtaining a considerable wage increase. Earlier, the Association had sued Alamos and won the case. All this contributed to the co-operative members' reluctance to adopt the discriminatory policies practiced by other co-operatives.

"We are paying them [temporary workers] all their benefits and bonuses. What other cooperatives are doing now is against the law. And it's better to do as the law says. If not, they may eventually fine you, so that you lose even more money that way. And then, how can we take away from these people [temporary workers]? They earn less than we do, and they always come to us, the stable ones, to ask for this or that. How can we leave them without health insurance? This would be sheer exploitation, worse then before: a peasant exploits a peasant." (field labourer)

Alamos' position on subdivision had not yet been clearly formulated. Subdivision had never been raised at the General Assembly, which, of course, did not prevent co-operative members from discussing it privately. During the interviews, six out of nineteen respondents at Alamos said that they favoured subdivision, and two expressed doubts. Given the satisfaction of all interviewed members with the internal co-operative organization and their awareness of the external causes of the crisis, the proportion of the supporters of subdivision seems surprisingly high. The interviews revealed two main motives for dissolving the production co-operative. First, while eighteen out of nineteen respondents would not agree that deteriorating labour discipline after land reform was the main cause of the crisis, five out of six pro-divisionists mentioned it as a minor evil that might be effectively eliminated by subdivision. Another reason, less frequently invoked but probably equally important, was a dramatic decrease in the co-operative members' incomes after retirement: a plot would nicely supplement a co-operative worker's meagre pension.

"If you ask me, subdivision is much better. Owning a plot, one would work with more endeavor. Instead of going out to the field at seven, one would go out at five, and not alone, but with the family. You know, all people are different. There are always some loafers around. These will go down after subdivision, no doubt about it. . . . Young people don't want subdivision either. They prefer to work from seven to twelve, and then go to town, to entertain themselves. Not us though [older people]. And what shall we gain after retirement? A pension and the shares we've paid to the co-operative, that's all. Of course, one of our children may join the co-operative, but for us there is nothing." (field labourer)

As for opponents of subdivision, their main argument was the shortage of water for irrigation. Almost all were afraid that those who got plots close to the co-operative wells would monopolize the irrigation de facto. In addition, many respondents referred to the lack of capital, which meant that they might have to mortgage their plots to obtain bank credit.

"Subdivision? No, I am against it. Land is not the same over here. . . . Some plots will come close to the wells and others will be far away. What if they give me a plot up there, where there is almost no water? Or what if those who have plots closer to the well will be irrigating all week and leave me with no water at all? Then what shall I do? Now it's different. The manager says: 'first we irrigate crops down here, then up there.' There is order, there is control." (field labourer)

These answers may be viewed as indicative of a purely technical limitation on subdivision. However, they also conveyed a clear recognition of the advantages of the collective organization of production in a situation of water scarcity.

SIGLO XX: MOBILIZATION AND REORGANIZATION

If Alamos could afford inaction, Siglo XX, whose economy was in disastrous shape, could not. Much of its members' energy was channelled into political pressure by national agrarian organizations. As already mentioned, Siglo XX was represented on the Executive Committee of the CNA and controlled the local Committee of Cotton Producers. It played an important role in regional co-operative mobilization and became directly involved in the organization of the Front for the Defence of Agriculture (other co-operatives were represented on it by the Agrarian League and the Committee of Cotton Producers). In contrast to Alamos, many members at Siglo XX shared a strong commitment to land reform and to the co-operative movement: "It will be a civil war, if *patrones* want their land back. It will be bloodshed, a real fight. . . . If you knew how they abused and mistreated people! We worked like draft animals, and they treated us like animals. Thanks to that general, Velasco, they were kicked out, and we will never let them back in again" (field labourer).

Similar attitudes, frequently supported by references to the recent land disputes, were expressed by other workers. Many had also participated actively in the national agrarian strikes in which Siglo XX played the usual leading role: "What else can we do with this government? We have no other choice left but to go on fighting. . . . Like we did with those two strikes. Two people were killed, and this seems to be the only thing left to us — to die fighting. There is no other way with this government" (field labourer).

This feeling, of course, was not unanimous. Some field labourers felt alienated from the regional mobilization in the same way that they felt alienated from the co-operative institutions: "We had to go because they [the administration] said that those who did not would be suspended for eight days. And what sort of strike was that? It was the leaders who called it; it was the managers. We went just because otherwise we would have been suspended" (field labourer).

Still, the predominant attitude seemed to be a readiness to exercise political pressure in defence of the co-operative property and economy. This readiness could be seen not only in Siglo XX's involvement in regional mobilization, but also in its skillful use of political connections in Lima. The most notable case was, of course, that of co-operative debt with ELECTROPERU, the state electric company. When energy to Siglo XX's wells was cut off in 1982 for the non-payment of electricity bills (see Chapter 6), the co-operative leaders used their political influence to talk with high-ranking officials of the Ministry of Energy and Mines, and eventually reached a compromise on extremely favourable terms. ELECTROPERU agreed to reschedule the co-operative debt, remitting the unpaid interest charges, and to change the industrial rate at which Siglo XX had been billed to the lower agro-industrial one.

Siglo XX combined political pressure with reorganization designed to reduce the co-operative's exorbitant spending. The measures were particularly harsh in the case of the co-operative's five hundred cotton pickers. Unlike Alamos, most cotton pickers at Siglo XX were unorganized seasonal migrants, which gave the co-operative administration a free hand in dealing with them. In 1981, the co-operative introduced new labour regulations involving the co-operative members in cotton picking along with temporary labourers. Each member formed a gang, hiring several hands. The hands were paid wages with no fringe benefits from funds allocated by the co-operative and based on the gang's output. This arrangement obviously benefitted the co-operative, which could now reduce temporary labour and eliminate temporary workers' fringe benefits. It was also designed to benefit individual co-operative members engaged in harvesting; for example, they themselves could decide how much to pay their hired hands or withhold their gang's holiday pay. Nevertheless, the measure raised immediate opposition inside the co-operative. To begin with, it fueled the long-standing conflict between the field labourers and the factory staff. The decision to engage co-operative workers in cotton picking involved the membership as a whole. Nevertheless, none of the skilled workers, not to mention the employees, took part in the harvest, to the indignation of the field labourers, who saw in the new arrangements another manifestation of intraco-operative inequalities. The field labourers' discontent was even greater, because many believed that the financial advantages which the new system offered to them did not compensate for the longer working day and the physical hardships involved in cotton picking.

"For us [co-operative members] it is not convenient to pick cotton. Now they are paying 1,850 *soles* for a quintal. And all one can do in a day is a quintal, a quintal and a half. So it's the same as the wages [we always get]. But for wages, one usually works from 7 to 12, and when picking cotton, one goes out at 5 and stays in the field till 3 or 4. Then, one must still weigh the cotton and take it to the factory. So, one comes back home at 6. It's thirteen hours altogether, and it's hard work, all day in the sun, having lunch in the field." (field labourer)

While the field labourers resented the desertion of the skilled workers, some of these, sincerely or not, accused the former of exploiting the temporary labourers: "It's the gang who are picking cotton, not the members. These gentlemen hire three, four, or five hands . . . and they do all the work. And they, the members, stay nearby looking at them. Just like former overseers!" (tractor driver). There was another, and probably even more serious, reason for the field labourers' discontent. Not only was the co-operative's decision viewed by many as unfair to seasonal migrants, it also directly affected their relatives who worked in the co-operative as temporary labourers. The opposition was especially strong in the *serrano* sector, whose members shared an ethnic identity with the seasonal migrants and whose wives were overwhelmingly involved in cotton picking and other heavy seasonal jobs which *costeño* women were generally unwilling to do. Actually, some dissident co-operative members openly sided with the temporary labourers, turning for advice to the General Confederation of Peruvian Workers (CGTP) and eventually taking the case to Labour Inspection. It visited Siglo XX, but found that the new system of recruitment did not contravene labour legislation.

While Siglo XX reduced expenditures on temporary labour, the intraco-operative reorganization was much more difficult to implement. The administration's attempt to freeze co-operative wages encountered bitter opposition among the workers, who used both general assemblies and trade union meetings to protest until the administration backed down and paid the increase demanded by the workers. The attempt to collect members' interest-free personal loans also failed. Finally, the co-operative adopted a so-called austerity program involving, among other things, the elimination of overtime and other extra payments (for night work, overtime on holidays), a more stringent control of factory transactions, and the suspension of some co-operative services (such as free electric service for domestic consumption and transportation subsidies for students). If the last of the three sets of measures did not cause much controversy, the first two were practically blocked by the skilled workers. The elimination of extra payments was opposed by the skilled workers (tractor and truck drivers, well operators, the electrical plant staff), who were generally on duty more than eight hours a day and who frequently worked on holidays. In the field sectors, the skilled workers were supported by those in charge of irrigation and night watch, who also received extra payments. After several weeks of complaints and negotiations, the administration was forced to return to the previous system of payments.

The tightening of internal controls proved to be even more controversial than the elimination of extra payments. The program envisaged additional controls over the use of gasoline and other co-operative supplies, an inventory of the warehouse, and the submission of weekly written reports by all factory shops with an account of the tasks performed by each skilled worker. The measures were supported by field labourers in general and by the workers of the remote sectors in particular. However, mistrusting administrative channels, they tended to use their own sectoral organizations for this purpose. Thus, the Defence Committee formed in 1981 by the *serrano* sector attempted to extend its activities from supervising potato harvesting to reviewing the factory books and inventorying the warehouse. The initiative was supported by the field labourers of the central sector. They also created a defence committee which, however, disintegrated rapidly under administrative pressure. The *serrano* defence committee persisted in its struggle for control, despite the refusal of the co-operative leadership to recognize the legitimacy of its claims.

Given the inadequacy and controversiality of both discussed strategies, it is not surprising that an increasing number of members started to question the usefulness of the existing co-operative structures, thus opening a debate on subdivision. In 1981, soon after the new Agrarian

Promotion Law permitted the restructuring of the agricultural production co-operatives, one Siglo XX employee proposed subdividing
the co-operative land to improve the members' individual work performance. The proposal was rejected by the General Assembly, yet
found many sympathizers. The following year witnessed a bitter
struggle between pro-divisionists and anti-divisionists. The core of
the anti-divisionist block was formed by younger skilled labourers
and employees of worker origins, grouped around the co-operative
PSR cell and closely linked to the Agrarian League and the CNA. They
used general assemblies and the co-operative's Education Committee
to expose the dangers of subdivision and even invited, with the same
objective, several high-ranking speakers from Lima (among them a
senator for the PSR). The co-operative also made a concession to the
advocates of subdivision: individual members were allotted spaces
between cotton rows where they could sow food corn.

Subdivision was debated at Siglo XX for over two years, at the end of
which its opponents seemed to win a sweeping victory. Forty-two out
of fifty-four respondents at Siglo XX were against subdivision. Interestingly, the proportion of anti-divisionists was lowest among members of
co-operative administration — the employees. One openly advocated
subdivision, four said that they had doubts, and only four others definitely rejected it. Among these four, three were younger office clerks,
and one was an overseer promoted after land reform. All singled out
government economic policies as the main source of the co-operative
crisis and favoured at least some forms of organization. Among the five
potential supporters of subdivision, four were overseers, and one was
an elderly office clerk. All five emphasized the role of labour discipline
and redundancy in the outbreak of the crisis, and all five were highly
critical of co-operative institutions (see Chapters 6 and 7).

As for manual workers, most of the skilled workers (nine out of ten)
and the field labourers (twenty-nine out of thirty-four) were against
subdivision. The number of opponents of subdivision among the
workers seemed to increase after the anti-divisionist campaign conducted by some members of the co-operative administration with the
support of the CNA. Undoubtedly, this campaign played an important
role in determining the final victory of the anti-divisionists. Its impact,
however, should not be overestimated. Most workers opposing subdivision developed the same arguments as their counterparts at Alamos, who had never been exposed to similar persuasion.

"I think it's better to work as we work now. If we divide the land, who will
control the water? And if I have no water on time, I shall lose my crop. And if I
lose my crop, the bank will take away my *parcela*. Or it may happen this way.

First, they will say: 'you have to pay 2,000 *soles* for the water.' And then, they will charge us 7,000 instead of 2,000. These people in the office can do anything. With money, it'll be also a problem. We'll have to ask for a bank loan, and the interest rate is very high. If it weren't for all this, I would say let's divide the land. Then everybody would have to work: there would be no loafing." (field labourer)

Many workers who rejected subdivision admitted that it still had two advantages: it would improve individual work performance, and it would also reduce the possibilities for mismanagement (even though, as argued in the following section, the opposite result was much more likely). For the five field worker supporters of subdivision, these advantages overshadowed all the possible disadvantages. One supporter, right after a description of co-operative mismanagement, gave this frank opinion:

"That's why my solution is subdivision. And mind you, people here wanted it, I mean all those who work in the field. But then someone brought a lawyer, and he discouraged them. Now they started saying, 'Who will control the water? Where shall we get money to work?' But I still believe it's better with the *parcela*. Then everybody would work differently. There would be no stealing either. . . . In the Sierra, everybody has *parcelas*, there are no co-operatives. People work for their family, not for the market. If you need help, here is *minka*, here is *ayni* [forms of communal labour practised by peasants in the Sierra]. That would be good. But here, on the coast, it is impossible. Pity." (field labourer)

Significantly, all five field labourers supporting subdivision were recent migrants from the Sierra, and in the course of the interview all made nostalgic remarks about their experiences back home. However, most *serrano* respondents, while sharing this nostalgia, agreed that those experiences were inapplicable to coastal agriculture.

Although subdivision did not gain much support among the workers, increased sectoral autonomy (*sectarización*) definitely did. Sectoral autonomy was advocated with particular fervour by field workers of the *serrano* sector represented by the Defence Committee. Feeling frustrated in their attempts to impose controls on the factory, they now proposed to transform each sector into an independent production co-operative or, at the very least, grant the field sectors a greater autonomy from the factory. Eleven out of fifteen respondents working in the remote sectors believed that such a measure would constitute a viable alternative to subdivision, curbing mismanagement without breaking collective production.

"You can't subdivide land in this co-operative. If I have a *parcela*, let's say here [he makes a drawing], and the well is there, I'd have to fight with this one, and this one, and this one, to get water for irrigation. . . . *Sectorización* is another thing. The co-operative has too many people. It's impossible to control what's happening here or there. We can't control from here what's going on at the factory. So, we'd rather split, so that they couldn't poke their nose here any more. If they want to steal, let them steal at the factory. But not here. What we have here should be ours." (field labourer)

Not surprisingly, most proponents of sectoral autonomy were internally oriented in their identification of the crisis, yet tended to favour at least some organizational activity.

MONTE BLANCO: REORGANIZATION AND SUBDIVISION

Unlike Siglo XX, Monte Blanco had no useful political and bureaucratic contacts in Lima. It also maintained a low profile in regional mobilization. Political pressure did not seem to have much appeal for its members, who became more concerned with the search for internal solutions to the co-operative's difficulties. Most cotton pickers at Monte Blanco were unorganized seasonal migrants, so that the first step taken by the co-operative administration in response to the crisis was the reintroduction of the pre-reform system of *enganche*. In 1981, cotton pickers were brought to the co-operative by a private contractor, the *enganchador*, who used his position of go-between to his own and the employer's advantage. Even though the co-operative had to pay a commission to the contractor, it could avoid health insurance and other fringe benefits payable to temporary workers under the written contracts.

The co-operative also stopped issuing written contracts to its forty quasi-temporary labourers. They lived in the same settlement as the stable labourers, and many were co-operative members' relatives, wives, and children. As a consequence, the abolition of written contracts affected co-operative members' families as well as those of temporary labourers, raising profound discontent among co-operative workers. However, this discontent did not result in open opposition, as it did at Siglo XX. Unlike Siglo XX, Monte Blanco had a long history of suppressing internal conflicts and avoiding contacts with national organizations questioning co-operative policies. In 1978, for instance, the quasi-temporary labourers, assisted by the Agrarian League, attempted to unionize to defend their wages. The co-operative administration, however, flatly refused to recognize the union and bitterly resented the League's interference in internal affairs. Confronted with the administration's intransigence, the union had gradually disintegrated, leaving the temporary labourers at its mercy.

In addition to modifying the recruitment system, Monte Blanco attempted to introduce austerity measures, such as an increase in working hours and a reorganization of the co-operative administration. In 1981, the General Assembly decided to extend the working day in the field from five to eight hours and to introduce unpaid work on Sundays, so that the co-operative could reduce the use of quasi-temporary labour. The new schedule lasted a week. As soon as a new loan came in from the bank, Monte Blanco returned to its usual practices.

Reorganization of the co-operative administration was proposed as early as 1980 by a ten-member commission made up mostly of present and former members of the co-operative administration. They recommended firing the co-operative manager and extending the number of members on the Administrative Council, including additional representatives from the field sectors. The co-operative hired a new manager, and the field sectors elected their representatives to the Council, but this did not seem to solve the financial problems. A year later, sixty-five co-operative members wrote an open letter demanding that the expanded Administrative Council resign.

Reorganization was interrupted by another initiative: a proposal to subdivide the co-operative. It came from the new manager, who outlined to the General Assembly the advantages of such a measure. The co-operative crisis, in his view, had been caused not by the unfavourable economic situation, but by the poor work performance of co-operative members. He argued that subdivision would permit the co-operative to reduce its swollen production costs in a number of ways. First, it would increase productivity (members, after becoming smallholders, were expected to work on their plots from sunrise to sunset). Second, it would permit the substitution of unpaid family work for hired temporary and quasi-temporary labour. Third, it would also encourage thrift towards agricultural inputs, water in particular. The Assembly, obviously convinced by this argument, elected a Commission on Subdivision which included the manager, a co-operative employee, and two co-operative leaders. A month later, the Commission submitted a report supporting the manager's proposal and even suggested a consulting firm to undertake the project. The report was approved and signed by seventy members, while twenty-two others abstained. Interestingly enough, among these twenty-two opponents of subdivision, only two were co-operative leaders and only one was an employee (the proportion of these categories in the total membership was much higher: of ninety-two members, fifteen were co-operative leaders and thirteen were employees). Yet six of them (27 per cent) were skilled workers, constituting only 18 per cent of the co-operative membership. Finally, sixteen out of twenty-two anti-divisionists — a clear majority — were younger, while the proportion of younger people in the co-operative as a whole was quite low because of its restrictive membership policies. While these data are certainly insufficient for drawing definite conclusions, they still indicate a pattern in the distribution of attitudes toward subdivision. It seems clear that the opposition to subdivision in Monte Blanco came mostly from manual workers in general, and from skilled and younger field labourers in particular. It is worth noting that skilled workers and younger members also played an important role in the anti-divisionist campaign in Siglo XX, and that these two groups, numerous at Siglo XX, were relatively small at Monte Blanco. As for the employees and co-operative leaders in Monte Blanco, they almost unanimously supported the Commission's recommendations.

In accordance with the project set up by the consulting firm and approved by the Assembly, the production co-operative at Monte Blanco was dissolved and replaced by a service co-operative. Most of the co-operative's irrigated lands (580 ha) was divided into plots (*parcelas*) of 6 ha on average (usually between 5 and 8 ha). The plots were distributed by lot among individual members — field labourers, skilled workers, and employees alike — who expected to own them after completing the required legal procedures. Each plot was valued on the basis of the market price of land and the cost of the crop growing on it at the time of subdivision. Their total value, however, also included the co-operative debt to the Agrarian Bank, which Monte Blanco had accumulated during the two previous growing seasons and which was now equally divided among all smallholders. The co-operative members undertook to cancel the total value over a number of years to the service co-operative, which was to mediate between them and the co-operative's creditors. The service co-operative also assumed some of the functions of its predecessor. It still owned 200 ha of irrigated lands worked by the smallholders without wages in exchange for health insurance. The service co-operative inherited the irrigation infrastructure as well as the machine pool, which it lent to its members. It was in charge of distributing agricultural inputs (water, fertilizers, pesticides, etc.) and marketing agricultural outputs. In addition, the co-operative provided its members with personal credit for their everyday needs (calculated on the basis of the former field wages) and for paying temporary workers during the harvest or other periods requiring additional labour.

All goods, services, and loans lent by the co-operative to each member during the growing season were to be repaid after harvest at the regular bank interest rate. It was not clearly stated what would happen to those who were unable to repay this short-term debt (plus the value of the plot). Most informants agreed that such "bad" members should be tolerated for some time, but eventually expelled from the co-operative and their land sold to one of the more successful members.

The immediate results of subdivision were rather contradictory and, on the whole, disappointing. The manager's argument about the change in individual work performance proved to be quite correct. Even though, in mid-1983, there were still no data on production costs after subdivision, the smallholders seemed highly likely, through thrift and hard work, to keep their production costs relatively low.

"You'll see, we are going to be better off next year. . . . The people work much better than before, with more willingness, with more endeavour. Temporary workers now get a job only in cases of emergency, because one has to pay them from one's own pockets. . . . Or take irrigation. Before, one woke up in the morning and found all the street [a passage between the fields] under water. Now, such things don't happen any more, people care about how much water they use." (assistant agronomist)

At the same time, subdivision had other, less beneficial, effects. First, it created technical problems. The fumigation of individual cotton fields, for instance, could not be adequately co-ordinated, which led to the spread of a cotton disease. Second, subdivision diminished the members' already low ability to control the co-operative administration. The smallholders still elected the Administrative and the Supervisory Councils, and occasionally held general assemblies, but their actual involvement in co-operative life fell dramatically: "People don't get together, don't talk as they used to. Everybody is toiling on the *parcelas*, nobody gives a damn about what's happening around. And nobody knows what's happening in the co-operative. The manager just doesn't inform us any more!" (field labourer).

From October 1982 to April 1983, the co-operative held no assemblies or any other general meetings. The elected administrative positions lost their attraction and importance:

"It's not worth the trouble being a [co-operative] leader now. The co-operative gives the president temporary workers only in cases of emergency. Otherwise, he has to take care of both the co-operative business and the *parcela*. . . . And other members of the [Administrative] Council just meet once a week.

Apart from this, they have nothing to do with the co-operative. As for the Supervisory Council, they don't even meet any more.... " (assistant agronomist)

Given members' disinterest in co-operative management, the question of who controlled the new service co-operative arose. Apparently, all important administrative decisions were made by the manager and the senior employees contracted by the co-operative. Since practically all co-operative members, including skilled workers and employees, became smallholders, the co-operative had to hire skilled workers from outside. The administrative core, however, remained very much the same: the manager (a non-member); the accountant (a non-member); and the chief overseer (a co-operative member who had held this position since pre-reform times). The most important role was played, of course, by the manager, who, significantly, ran his own business as a distributor of fertilizers and pesticides, and who sold them lavishly (and at his own price) to the co-operative under his administration.

Given the record of mismanagement at Monte Blanco, the increased decisional autonomy of the senior administrative staff seemed likely to open new possibilities for manipulating the co-operative economy to favour private interests. In other words, the gains which smallholders might achieve through hard work and thrift would probably be wiped out by the appropriative practices of the co-operative management.

Finally, and most importantly, subdivision triggered socio-economic differentiation far exceeding, in scope and implications, the limited differentiation inside the production co-operative. To begin with, not all plots were the same size and quality or had similar access to irrigation canals. Moreover, at the time of subdivision, they were all sown with different crops, some of which were more profitable than others. At the end of the season, the users of plots with wheat, sorghum, barley, and industrial corn had heavy losses which further increased their debts to the co-operative. The individual cotton producers had neither profits nor losses, and the potato growers made handsome profits, being able to repay a good part of their total debt to the co-operative. All this raised a controversy about the position of the co-operative on losses in cereals. The cereal producers (twenty-nine in total) argued that since the co-operative had sown the cereals, it should also assume the losses, while the other members insisted that these were the personal responsibility of the smallholders. The second point of view prevailed, which meant that at least twenty-nine co-operative members became the most likely candidates for losing their land.

These developments increased the number of the opponents of subdivision who now demanded a return to the previous co-operative organization. However, they lacked the political experience and external support which played such an important role in the anti-divisionist victory at Siglo XX. Many felt that they had been cheated and manipulated by their own administration but were unable to break their traditional political isolation. Even more importantly, most co-operative members at Monte Blanco had accepted the subdivision, despite the technical, organizational, and economic problems involved. Why?

The reasons varied with the respondents' position in the co-operative. Five out of the six interviewed workers wanted to subdivide the co-operative lands to rid themselves of the co-operative employees. In this way, they hoped to end the corruption and inequalities of which, in their opinion, they had been victims since the co-operative was organized: "Of course it's better to work with a *parcela*. Don't you see how much stealing goes on in [production] co-operatives? With a *parcela*, it's different. One wakes up early, goes to work with his wife, his children. . . . And all that the land yields now belongs to him." (field labourer).

By contrast, the interviewed members of co-operative administration argued in accordance with the "official" version that subdivision was necessary to increase agricultural labour productivity. However, this apparent concern with economic performance cloaked the anticipation of certain individual benefits denied to this category of members under the production co-operative's arrangements. What might these benefits have been? Among office clerks, it might have been the prospect of liberation from the eight-hour working day. Staying in the office, they frequently missed business opportunities opened to them during their co-operative administrative career. Unwilling to forsake their salaries, they were still looking for new arrangements enabling them to dedicate more time to their lucrative sidelines.

"Personally, I prefer to work with a *parcela*. I have worked in the office almost all my life. And this way one has a lot of opportunities for meeting all sorts of people, for making useful contacts. Now, after subdivision, I have to work in the co-operative only two days a week. As to the rest of it, I can either work on the *parcela*, or look after my business [probably in town]. Before, I had to stay in the co-operative eight hours every day, and what you earn like that is not enough for a living." (office clerk)

The administrative staff in general might also have anticipated land redistribution in their favour. Having accumulated certain resources (material wealth, contacts, information) in operating the production co-operative, they generally felt optimistic about their future as private land owners. The actual reasons for this optimism, however, were usually disguised by the rhetoric of thrift and hard work.

"It's better with subdivision. Of course some people are going to have problems. . . . Some are loafers, others like to drink or go to fiestas. These, for sure, won't be able to pay their debts. So, they will have to hand over their plots to those who work well. They have no right to sell them outside the co-operative, because the co-operative owns the infrastructure. Many people will fall out this way. Who knows, maybe at the end there will be only thirty or forty of us left." (co-operative leader)

Ironically, this co-operative leader was a founder and the first president of the production co-operative at Monte Blanco. Only two out of the fourteen respondents (both skilled workers) opposed subdivision. As a consequence of subdivision, both lost their skilled jobs in the co-operative without having much to start private businesses. Both argued that subdivision adversely affected the manual workers' ability to defend their interests. And both were painfully aware of their own isolation and inability to change events.

CONCLUSION

The co-operatives' responses to the crisis varied considerably, depending on their socio-economic and political characteristics. The least defined pattern of behaviour was found at Alamos, which should not be surprising, given the relative levity of the economic crisis here. When I was conducting my field research, Alamos seemed to be weighing various options, postponing painful decisions and watching other co-operatives' struggles and agonies. However, if the economic situation continues to worsen, Alamos could be forced into action. In this case, political mobilization looks the least likely option to be adopted, for it definitely goes against the co-operative's deeply rooted tradition of organizational autonomy and political noninvolvement. The situation might change if the younger workers, more politically oriented than the founders of the co-operative, increase their internal influence. If this does not happen, Alamos is likely to continue standing apart from the national co-operative movement. The second possible option, reorganization, does not look feasible either: co-operative expenses at Alamos are already extraordinarily low, and their further reduction, even at the expense of the temporary labourers, would be subject to serious social constraints. This leaves Alamos with one last option: subdivision. The idea of subdividing such a well-organized, efficient co-operative as Alamos sounds almost absurd, but many members concluded privately that this is the most desirable solution to the co-operative's economic difficulties.

At Siglo XX and Monte Blanco the economic crisis was more intense and their members' responses were more clearly defined than were those at Alamos. However, while Siglo XX was looking for collective solutions to its economic difficulties (political mobilization among them), Monte Blanco opted for subdivision. Why?

As argued in previous chapters, both co-operatives organized by the state had preserved their pre-reform occupational structure, simultaneously incorporating a large number of quasi-temporary labourers and, in the case of Monte Blanco, small tenants. This created extremely heterogeneous memberships whose level of educational and organizational experience did not always correspond to the level of the co-operatives' entrepreneurial complexity. As a result, Siglo XX and Monte Blanco failed to develop viable co-operative institutions which emerged "naturally" in the small, socially homogeneous Alamos. Moreover, the state-sponsored co-operatives developed marked socio-economic inequalities largely because of private economic activities and bureaucratic forms of administration. Both phenomena were conducive to deteriorating individual work performance and mismanagement, which added to the negative effects of the government economic policies. In this situation, a political mobilization designed to change these policies did not appear as the only effective strategy for the economic crisis. Another was internal reorganization, attempted at both Siglo XX and Monte Blanco. However, since most co-operative members had vested interests in the status quo, reorganization did not go beyond cutbacks in spending on temporary and quasi-temporary labour. The general ineffectiveness of the co-operatives' "austerity plans," in turn, raised the question of the subdivision, which promised to reduce the swollen production costs and administrative expenses. At the same time, it offered private land ownership to co-operative workers whose co-operative incomes were threatened by the economic crisis. As such, it was welcomed by many co-operative members as an alternative to both political pressure and reorganization within the production co-operative.

This explanation, emphasizing the economic rationality of subdivision, was frequently invoked by supporters of subdivision inside and outside the co-operatives. A closer look at the internal workings of co-operatives, however, suggests that it is far from being totally satisfactory. It overlooks the role of private interests in contriving subdivision, as well as the existence of a partly rational discontent among field labourers, skilfully exploited by these interests. The similar discontent at Siglo XX and Monte Blanco stemmed from the persistence of socio-economic inequalities and the inefficiency of participatory structures following land reform. Tinged by resentment and frustration, it evolved, in some cases, into a rejection of any form of co-operation and a glorification of economic individualism. However, the outbursts of such blind anti-co-operativism among field labourers were not the immediate cause of subdivision. Initiative generally came from members of the co-operative administration, that is, those who effectively benefited from the inequalities. Owing to their administrative positions, some developed considerable private economies inside and outside the co-operative, sometimes in conjunction with local commercial interests or state bureaucracies. These economics could be expected to gain more momentum after the private distribution of the lands of the production co-operatives already mired in an economic crisis. This happy coincidence of private interest and concern with the swollen co-operative production costs turned many members of the co-operative administration at Siglo XX and Monte Blanco into arduous advocates of subdivision. Ironically, their advocacy found a positive response among their long-standing opponents, the discontented field labourers, who chose to join them in the newly formed pro-divisionist coalition.

Such a coalition was formed at both Monte Blanco and Siglo XX. However, while at Monte Blanco it included most co-operative members, at Siglo XX it failed to gain similar strength. Three interrelated sets of factors account for these different outcomes. One has to do with the organization of production on the pre-reform haciendas (see Chapter 4). Before land reform, Siglo XX was a centralized agro-industrial entreprise with a large stable labour force. As a consequence, most of its co-operative membership was made up of stable labourers with a relatively long history of wage-earning. Even if the labourers shared discontent with intraco-operative inequalities and blamed the economic crisis on the co-operative administration, they were still reluctant to dismantle the system of production which was giving them relative economic security. By contrast, Monte Blanco had operated as a partly decentralized hacienda relying on quasi-temporary labour in its centrally managed area. Therefore, most of its members were quasi-temporary labourers or small tenants who, from their experiences, felt less apprehensive about individual production than their counterparts at Siglo XX.

The differences in pre-reform economic experiences were reinforced by differences in the scope and nature of private economic activities after land reform, which also influenced the relative success of the pro-divisionist coalitions. As argued in Chapter 4, both Siglo XX and Monte Blanco became plagued by the development of complementary private economic activities based on co-operative resources. At Monte Blanco, however, the scope of these activities was much larger than at Siglo XX. Moreover, they were related primarily to family agriculture practised within the co-operative. This fact reflected the difficulties involved in the post-reform centralization of agricultural production, which, in turn, could be largely explained by the hacienda's inadequate system of irrigation wells. The persistence of family agriculture was also related to the availability of water from the local river, which diminished the producers' dependence on the co-operative-owned irrigation wells. The extraordinary (for a production co-operative) development of family agriculture at Monte Blanco minimized its members' reliance on co-operative incomes, facilitating the formal transition from collective to individual production involved in the subdivision of co-operative lands.

The third set of factors has to do with the post-reform operation of co-operative institutions (see Chapter 5). In both state-sponsored co-operatives, these institutions became controlled by the co-operative bureaucracy engaged in lucrative private activities. At Siglo XX, however, bureaucratization was accompanied by internal and external politicization, which facilitated the workers' pressure for social and economic benefits and increased their awareness of the external causes of the crisis. Furthermore, politicization manifested itself in the emergence of a group of worker-leaders and younger employees of worker origins who effectively challenged the co-operative bureaucracy. In the 1980s, this opposition group, supported by the CNA, played an important role in counteracting the bureaucracy's attempts to contrive subdivison. By contrast, the co-operative bureaucracy at Monte Blanco suppressed all forms of worker participation and prevented the strong ties with the national co-operative movement. As a consequence, the co-operative workers were not only less successful in obtaining social and economic benefits than their counterparts at Siglo XX, but also less aware of the policy-related nature of the crisis. Moreover, they failed to produce a cohesive, influential opposition leadership which could have carried out the anti-divisionist campaign, so important in the case of Siglo XX.

CHAPTER EIGHT

Conclusion

The analysis of agricultural co-operative experience in Peru indicates that it has been closely related to national historical change. The failure of Peruvian agricultural co-operatives to develop into self-sustained units through co-operative principles reflected not so much an inherent irrelevance of these principles in the non-Western world — as some students of rural co-operativism have argued — but rather their inapplicability in the particular historical situation which gave rise to Peruvian agricultural co-operativism. The peculiarities of this situation accounted for the emergence of a co-operative movement very different from the European and North American models. Compared with these models, the Peruvian co-operative movement was certainly a failure, but not necessarily a failure in its own right.

The co-operative movement in Peru developed on a national scale during military populism characterized by increased state intervention in national economic development. Most agricultural production co-operatives were created directly by the state, on which they came to depend administratively, economically, and politically. Such state-sponsored production units certainly had little in common with independent grassroots forms of co-operation generally identified with the concept of co-operativism. Their emergence and operation were determined by state policies rather than by the spontaneous actions of direct agricultural producers who had opted for co-operation of their own free will. As a consequence, an analysis of state policies for the co-operative agricultural sector is extremely important for understanding its functioning.

There is a danger, though, in placing too much emphasis on the role of state policies in the analysis of co-operative development. As shown in the previous discussion, actual co-operative practices were determined as much by co-operative members' responses to these policies as by the policies themselves. These responses sometimes went as far as to imply a total rejection of state interference with the co-operative movement. More frequently, however, they involved co-operative members' attempts to turn this interference to their own collective or individual advantage. The result was a co-operative movement which differed considerably not only from independent, spontaneous forms of co-operation, but also from the image of state-controlled, exploitative, and manipulative co-operativism depicted by some students of Peruvian rural politics.

To be sure, the state bureaucracy tried to bring the co-operative movement under its control. However, this effort was repeatedly frustrated by the co-operative members' pursuit of collective and individual gains, a pursuit which considerably modified the co-operative arrangements imposed on them. Thus, agricultural co-operative structures in Peru became "distorted" twice: first, through state intervention in co-operative development; and second, through co-operative members' attempts to adjust the state-sponsored co-operative system to their needs and interests.

The first distortion reflected basically the historical conditions under which agricultural co-operativism in Peru had developed. As already mentioned, it emerged as a national movement during military populism characterized by increased state intervention in the national economy. The military populist government implemented import-substitution industrialization (ISI) policies in combination with a land reform program designed to increase the supply of cheap domestic agricultural commodities to the growing urban-industrial sectors.

Most agricultural co-operatives organized by the state were expropriated capitalist or semi-capitalist haciendas. In the cotton-growing sector, the main object of my research, the capitalist haciendas had developed in connection with the local and Andean peasant sectors which provided them with cheap quasi-temporary and temporary labour. By transforming these haciendas into state-controlled production co-operatives, the military populist government intended to preserve (or improve) their economic efficiency and, at the same time, to increase their contribution to the national textile industry. If fully implemented, this strategy would have produced a co-operative sector with restricted membership (limited basically to the stable hacienda labour force), pronounced occupational and income inequalities, and bureaucratic co-operative institutions. The actual co-operative practices, however, did not exactly correspond to the state-controlled model.

It is true that cotton production co-operatives were based on the hacienda system, reinforcing the functional dualism between the capitalist and the peasant sectors which had developed prior to land reform. Nevertheless, as the case studies show, the state-sponsored co-operatives absorbed a considerable number of local semi-proletarianized peasants employed on cotton haciendas as quasi-temporary labourers or small tenants. Incorporating these two categories of labour into the production co-operatives was particularly significant on cotton haciendas which had a relatively small centralized area and which relied heavily on quasi-temporary, rather than on stable, labour. To some extent, this incorporation reflected the contradictory nature of the government co-operative policies, designed to promote large-scale units of production yet spread the economic benefits of co-operation to the semi-proletarianized peasants excluded from land redistribution. More importantly, however, it was conducted in response to pressure from the quasi-temporary hacienda labour force, who expected to improve their incomes by obtaining stable jobs in the production co-operatives.

The incorporation of quasi-temporary labourers and small tenants into the post-reform co-operative system was not sufficiently significant to change the peasant sector at large. However, as the case studies of the two state-sponsored co-operatives (Siglo XX and Monte Blanco) demonstrate, it had a profound effect on the co-operative sector itself. First, it increased the haciendas' stable labour force, inflating the co-operatives' payroll and raising their production costs. Second, it brought in small agricultural producers with narrow collective experience to the co-operative units based on collective production. This hampered worker participation in management, which required co-operative members to have a certain familiarity with centralized hacienda production, as well as minimal organizational skills. Significantly, the independent co-operative (Alamos), which most closely approximated the spontaneous form of rural co-operation, was based on a capitalist hacienda with a very high proportion of stable workers in its permanent labour force. Its co-operative members were recruited almost exclusively among the unionized stable workers with a long experience of collective work, which certainly contributed to its success as a co-operative. (The differences and similarities in the development of the three co-operatives studied are summarized in Table 25.)

The pressure from the hacienda labour force not only expanded the social boundaries of the state-sponsored co-operative sector, but also modified its organizational make-up. Conceived as a complement for the ISI policies, the 1969 land reform preserved the occupational hierarchy on expropriated haciendas and established state controls on

TABLE 25: Patterns of co-operative development at Alamos, Siglo XX, and Monte Blanco

	Alamos	Siglo XX	Monte Blanco
Role of state in organization of co-operatives	marginal	central	central
Type of pre-reform hacienda	centrally managed	centrally managed	decentralized
Predominant type of wage labour force prior to land reform	stable	stable/temporary	temporary
Socio-economic differentiation among co-operative members	low	high	high
Informal privatization of co-operative economy	low	moderate	high
Bureaucratization of co-operative institutions	low	high	high
Politicization of co-operative institutions	low	high	low
Co-operative economic efficiency	high	low	low
Co-operative economic crisis	moderate	severe	severe
Co-operative responses to crisis	uncertain	political pressure reorganization	subdivision

their administration. These policies brought about high levels of intraco-operative income differentials and bureaucratized co-operative administrative institutions. These phenomena, however, cannot be explained by state action alone. In both state-sponsored co-operative studied, state intervention triggered socio-economic differentiation and bureaucratization, which tended to escape state controls; it produced co-operative organization, which seemed to have as little in common with the state-controlled model of co-operativism as it had with the spontaneous forms of co-operation.

First, even though the government tried to maintain the co-operatives' economic efficiency by establishing wage controls, these controls did not seem to be very effective. Despite the government stabilization programs and the high rates of inflation after the demise of military populism, real agricultural wages in the three state-sponsored co-operatives studied climbed, pushing up the co-operatives' production costs and increasing their reliance on short-term state agricultural credit. This growth outpaced the increase in both the salaries of co-operative technical-administrative staff (the employees) and the wages of skilled co-operative workers. As a consequence, even though the hacienda occupational hierarchy remained virtually intact, the intraco-operative wage differentials tended to level off. Curiously, the agricultural wages in the independent co-operative grew much more slowly than they did in the state-sponsored ones. To some extent, this could be explained by its members' concern with the profitability of the co-operative enterprise, as well as their reluctance to increase their dependence on state credit. Also, equalizing wages within the co-operative reduced the field workers' pressure for higher pay.

The relatively high agricultural wages in the state-sponsored co-operatives were complemented by a wide range of social services: elementary schooling, adult education, co-operative transportation, health services, etc. The co-operative services benefitted all co-operative members, especially the field workers. Along with the relatively high agricultural wages, the services swelled co-operative expenditures and decreased formal income differentials among co-operative members. This decrease, however, failed to prevent internal conflicts, generally associated with high socio-economic inequalities, largely because differentiation suppressed in formal co-operative incomes and benefits reappeared in private economic activities. These activities varied. Some technical-administrative staff tried to offset the trend toward equalization by using their key positions in co-operative production for private gains. This phenomenon, known mostly as co-operative mismanagement, gave rise to various private agricultural and commercial enterprises based on co-operative resources. By contrast, the complementary economic activities among field workers followed the logic of family subsistence, involving work on plots which most hacienda workers and tenants retained or acquired after joining production co-operatives.

Private economic activities in the state-sponsored co-operatives, Siglo XX and Monte Blanco, diminished members' collective work performance, and increased the co-operatives' productive and non-productive expenditures while exacerbating internal conflicts. The independent co-operative, Alamos, successfully avoided these problems by restricting socio-economic differentiation in both formal co-operative incomes and private activities. The success of Alamos' strategy was determined, to some extent, by its labour force being composed almost exclusively of stable workers. However, it could also be explained by the virtual elimination of the category of co-operative employees and by the effective operation of co-operative administrative institutions, which contrasted sharply with the bureaucratic management typical of the state-sponsored co-operatives, Siglo XX and Monte Blanco.

To a large extent, bureaucratization in the post-reform co-operative sector developed because of a gap between the managerial complexity of the state-sponsored production co-operatives and the technical and organizational skills among most of the membership. This gap could be seen in both state-sponsored co-operatives studied, where the General Assembly failed to effectively channel worker participation into co-operative management. Moreover, the elected co-operative leadership (the Administrative Council) were likely to be recruited from the co-operative technical-administrative staff (the employees). Even when they were in a minority on the Council, the employees tended to dominate co-operative decisionmaking because of their technical expertise. As a consequence, the co-operatives' decisionmaking core merged with the occupational one, giving rise to the so-called co-operative bureaucracy, as represented by the co-operative employees and the co-opted worker-leaders. The co-operative bureaucrats found allies among state officials employed in the local branches of the Ministry of Agriculture, the Agrarian Bank, and the state marketing agencies. In the absence of effective worker control, these two categories of local bureaucrats seemed to be quite successful in manipulating the co-operative economy in their own interests, imposing on it the logic of private accumulation.

Thus, the bureaucratization of post-reform co-operatives was caused not only by the state control of co-operative management, but also by the peculiarities of the socio-economic structures on which they had been superimposed. The complex entrepreneurial forms of capitalist agriculture and the poorly organized and poorly educated labour force created the preconditions for the subsequent bureaucratization, which facilitated the development of private interests within the co-operatives and institutionalized co-operative mismanagement. This, however, was not the only consequence of co-operative bureaucracy. In some cases, the trend toward bureaucratizing co-operative institutions generated a countertrend — a trend for their politicization.

As my field research shows, in only one of the two state-sponsored co-operatives (Monte Blanco) did the bureaucracy gain an almost unchallenged control of the administration. In the other (Siglo XX), the General Assembly and the Administrative Council became a battlefield on which the co-operative bureaucracy and the opposition worker-leaders struggled for power. This struggle reflected what could be called the internal politicization of co-operative institutions. The growth of co-operative bureaucracy prevented effective worker participation in co-operative administration, diverting workers' concerns into immediate economic benefits, and making them act, to a large extent, with a trade union mentality. This behaviour, however, became intertwined with the workers' attempts to gain control of co-operative management. As a consequence, worker participation at Siglo XX acquired an essentially political character, which distinguished it not only from the democratic management practiced at the independent Alamos, but also from the unchallenged rule of bureaucracy in the other state-sponsored co-operative, Monte Blanco.

Trade union experience prior to land reform seemed to be a precondition for this politicized form of intraco-operative participation. Clearly, the high internal politicization was typical of a co-operative formed from a capitalist estate with a great many stable unionized workers in its total labour force. By contrast, the development of co-operative bureaucracy on the hacienda relying on quasi-temporary labour and tenancy failed to generate the countertrend toward internal politicization.

The trend toward internal politicization in state-sponsored co-operatives was complemented by a trend toward their external politicization. The post-reform co-operative movement was created by the military-populist government as an alternative to independent rural organization. It developed under the control of the state bureaucracy, as represented by SINAMOS, within an inclusionary-corporatist institutional framework. However, the state political controls not only inhibited the development of independent political orientations among the hacienda workers, but also increased their sensitivity to political issues, linking the problem of local co-operative development to that of national political change. Moreover, within the inclusionary-corporatist framework, the state-sponsored co-operative movement enjoyed a certain political autonomy, reflected in the CNA's early attempts to influence government agricultural policies. This autonomy turned into political independence after the demise of military populism. Under the independent CNA leadership, the co-operative movement challenged the exclusionary-corporatist arrangements of the post-populist military regime and organized opposition to the increasingly neo-liberal agricultural policies after the return to civilian rule.

The co-operatives' participation in the national co-operative movement reflected their external politicization. As with the internal politicization, the participation was particularly effective in the co-operative formed from a capitalist hacienda with a relatively large, unionized, stable labour force. On this hacienda, state-sponsored co-operativism expanded the workers' concerns into the realm of state agricultural policies. This expansion, however, did not take place on the hacienda with a high proportion of non-unionized, quasi-temporary labourers and tenants. After land reform, the workers on this hacienda remained politically passive, showing little interest either in government agricultural policies or in the CNA-led co-operative mobilization. Thus, to a very large extent, the post-reform co-operative movement represented a continuation of, rather than an alternative to, the independent trade union movement.

As far as I could see, the actual co-operative practices in Peru differed considerably from the state-controlled model of co-operativism sometimes presented in the literature. The socially restrictive character of post-reform co-operatives was modified by a massive incorporation of local semi-proletarianized peasants. Income differentials were more or less effectively suppressed in formal co-operative incomes and benefits. They reappeared, however, in private economic activities. Finally, the trend toward the bureaucratization of co-operative institutions, which facilitated the development of these activities, gave rise to a countertrend toward their politicization. These peculiarities of Peruvian co-operativism accounted for a complex nature of co-operative economic crisis which triggered the dissolution of the post-reform co-operative sector.

The crisis was caused, to a large extent, by the change in national economic strategies after the demise of military populism. Under the post-populist regimes, the state-sponsored ISI policies gave way to economic orthodoxy, with emphasis on private entreprise and a closer integration of the national economy with the world capitalist system. The post-populist policy of exchange rate adjustment escalated the cost of agricultural inputs, pushing up production costs. This policy was complemented by the elimination of tax and credit incentives for co-operative agriculture. In the cotton-growing sector, the negative effect of these policies was amplified by the preservation of the state monopoly of the cotton trade, which benefitted the domestic textile industry. This combination of the post-populist exchange, credit, and price policies accounted for the financial difficulties experienced by cotton co-operatives in the early 1980s. These difficulties, however, were augmented by the growth of the co-operatives' productive and administrative expenditures related to the increased stable labour force and to its success in obtaining a wide range of formal and informal economic benefits. As a consequence, the co-operative economic crisis had external and internal causes. As such, it tended to evoke among co-operative members two — or rather three — different responses.

One response corresponding to the policy-related nature of the crisis, was the participation in the CNA-led co-operative mobilization against agricultural policies. This response was a search for an external solution to the co-operative crisis. The other two responses related to the internal aspect of the crisis and sought internal solutions. One was the implementation of internal measures designed to increase the economic efficiency of the production co-operatives. The other, encouraged by the national government as part of the neo-liberal counter-reform, was the subdivision of the co-operative lands. While the first two responses to the crisis implied the preservation of collective production, the third involved the dissolution of production co-operatives and the transfer of co-operative lands to the individual ownership of their members.

The case studies showed that the economic crisis was much more intense in the state-sponsored co-operatives, and so was the search for external and/or internal solutions. This search, however, did not lead inevitably to a subdivision of co-operative lands. Both state-sponsored co-operatives tried alternative solutions, and only one (Monte Blanco) eventually opted for subdivision. Thus, it would be wrong to assume that the distortion of the co-operative structures by state intervention caused an unambiguous rejection among the co-operative membership. Plainly, the co-operative agricultural workers obtained considerable economic benefits within the state-sponsored co-operative sector. Their discontent was centered primarily on the skewed distribution of benefits caused by the success of the co-operative bureaucracy in using the collective economy to its own advantage. This discontent, rather than discontent with the state co-operative policies as such, made them question the validity of collective production. Even so, this questioning was not necessarily translated into an advocacy of subdivision. In both state-sponsored co-operatives, the initiative in subdivision did not come from dissatisfied field workers, but from the well-to-do members of the co-operative bureaucracy who intended to use it for augmenting their private means.

The important role played by the privately oriented co-operative bureaucrats in contriving subdivision indicates that the anti-co-operative movement of the 1980s had a close affinity with the attempts of the small and medium agrarian bourgeoisie to use the post-populist national strategies for improving their economic and political status. The co-operative field workers supported subdivision to the extent that they were dissatisfied with the distribution of benefits within the co-operatives. However, they were not entirely ready to exchange the benefits available to them within this system for the uncertainties of individual production. The outcome of workers' doubts depended on factors related to the organization of production on the haciendas in question.

One factor was the social composition of the co-operative member-ship, as determined by the levels of managerial centralization and the structure of the wage labour force on the pre-reform haciendas. As already noted, some state-sponsored production co-operatives were formed from decentralized haciendas or the haciendas dependent on quasi-temporary labour provided by the local smallholding sectors. The membership in such co-operatives was made up of former small ten-ants and quasi-temporary labourers whose links with the land has been much stronger than was those of the stable workers. Accordingly, their members were more susceptible to subdivision than the members of co-operatives formed from centrally managed haciendas relying on stable labour.

The second factor had to do with private economic activities in general, and family agriculture in particular, within the production co-operatives. Partly they reflected production on pre-reform haciendas: family agriculture was more likely to develop on previously decentral-ized haciendas. This development, however, was also related to the post-reform privatization of the co-operative economy, triggered by the co-operative members' search for complementary incomes. The grow-ing importance of these incomes vis-à-vis the co-operative benefits eroded by the economic crisis diminished both the workers' reliance on collective production and their commitment to co-operative organiza-tion.

A third factor was workers' attitudes toward subdivision, reflecting the levels of internal and external politicization of co-operative institu-tions. These levels tended to be particularly high on centrally managed haciendas dependent on unionized stable labour. After land reform, and especially after the co-operative crisis began, the trade union tradition was transformed into co-operative political militancy. This militancy manifested itself inside the co-operatives in workers' opposition to the co-operative bureaucracy and, on the regional/national levels, in the workers' participation in co-operative political mobilization. The political experiences inside and outside the co-operatives had profound implications for the workers' position on subdivision. Even though the internal politicization reflected a failure to establish an effective worker control on co-operative management, it permitted agricultural workers to obtain higher co-operative wages and better social services, increasing their "pragmatic" commitment to co-operative organization. Moreover, it also made possible the introduction of more democratic forms of management within the production co-operatives, preventing a total alienation of the workers from the co-operative institutions. The internal politicization of workers' attitudes toward subdivision was reinforced by external politicization, expressed in close ties between the co-operative membership and the regional and national CNA leaders. These ties facilitated the CNA's efforts to increase the workers' awareness of the benefits inherent in the co-operative system and to direct their attention to the policy-related causes of the crisis.

Clearly, state intervention in the co-operative movement created both the preconditions for subdivision and its antidote. It facilitated the development of the co-operative bureaucracy which imposed the logic of private appropriation on the co-operative economy, different not only from that of the co-operative but also from that of state-controlled co-operativism. At the same time, it provided the rural labour force with considerable economic and social benefits and created new forms of local and national political participation, exceeding in scope both participation in co-operative management and trade union economic struggles.

The co-operatives' response to the crisis depended on the relative weight of each set of factors. The trend toward the informal privatization of the co-operative economy gave rise to the movement for subdividing co-operative lands in support of the neo-liberal economic policies. The trend toward an increased worker economic and political participation within the co-operative system was responsible for their members' predisposition to defend it against these policies. Thus, even though the state-sponsored co-operatives failed as co-operatives, they succeeded as state-created mass organizations, which improved the economic position of the rural labour force and changed the national and local balance of power.

The analysis of the Peruvian co-operative movement also sheds light on some of the more general theoretical issues discussed in Chapter 1. One set of questions raised by this analysis concerns changes in agrarian social structures following land reforms. As argued by de Janvry and Ground (1978), most land reforms in Latin America (including Peru) did not represent a radical break with the capitalist transformation of agriculture based on cheap temporary labour. Rather, the reforms either accelerated this transformation, or produced a shift from the junker to the farmer road of transition to capitalist agriculture, as was the case with the 1969 land reform in Peru. Nowhere did they eliminate the functional dualism between the capitalist and peasant sectors typical of Latin American agrarian structures.

These conclusions, however, need certain qualifications. First, the transformation of Peru's coastal estates into agricultural production co-operatives limited private agriculture to the non-reform sector (even though in many cases family farming continued to exist, de facto, within the production co-operatives). More importantly, this transformation involved not only large centrally managed haciendas, but also decentralized and small centrally managed estates (the latter were usually incorporated into larger estates). As a result, a large number of small tenant farms and medium capitalist production units became part of the large-scale centrally managed entreprises. This suggested that, rather than promoting farmer agriculture, the 1969 land reform reinforced a large-scale, if not a junker, pattern of transition to capitalist agriculture.

Second, organizing agricultural production co-operatives out of the decentralized coastal haciendas was complemented by incorporating some quasi-temporary labourers (local independent smallholders) into the co-operative stable labour force. This led to an expansion of wage relations not only vis-à-vis the relations of tenancy, but also — and even more significantly — vis-à-vis the local peasant economy. The latter consideration is particularly important. It implies that even though functional dualism in the coastal region remained basically unchanged, the weight of the large-scale agricultural sector increased in comparison with the local peasant sector. Third, land reform also brought qualitative changes to the former capitalist sector. A considerable portion of it was reorganized by the state along co-operative lines. Introducing co-operative institutions on expropriated haciendas complicated the capitalist relations of production and appropriation — another consideration to be taken into account in analysing the social implications of land reforms.

The land reform conducted by the military-populist regime expanded large-scale agrarian capitalism in a state-co-operative version. The neo-liberal counter-reform that followed the demise of military populism triggered changes in the opposite direction. The subdivision of co-operative lands on the coast implied a substitution of small holdings for large-scale co-operative production. Some new smallholders (those with better lands and access to additional resources) could be expected to develop into successful capitalist farmers. Others, unable to cover production and subsistence expenses, might be forced to sell their lands and migrate to the cities, thereby augmenting the already sizeable marginal urban population. Still others would probably remain in the countryside as smallholders providing cheap temporary or quasi-temporary labour for the local capitalist sector. As a consequence, large-scale agriculture on the coast was likely to shrink, giving both the capitalist farmer and the peasant sectors room to grow. Whether this land deconcentration will be only temporary depends on factors beyond the scope of this book. It should be noted, though, that the international market and government economic policies will be critical in this respect. An expansion of export agriculture in accordance with neo-liberal economic prescriptions might reconcentrate land, probably upon the initiative of transnational commercial and agro-industrial capital.

Another set of questions raised by the analysis of Peruvian cotton co-operativism is related to the problem of agricultural policies in general, and price policies in particular, used by the state in promoting industrial growth. From the nationalization of the cotton trade in 1974 to its privatization in 1983, cotton prices in Peru benefitted the textile interests at the expense of the cotton producers. Domestic cotton prices were set far below the international levels. Moreover, their increase tended to lag behind cotton production costs pushed up by the rise in the prices of imported and domestically produced agricultural inputs and consumer goods. These trends indicate that Lipton's notion of "price twists" (Lipton 1977) is applicable to the relations between the Peruvian cotton-growing and textile sectors during the period in question, even though the situation with other crops (e.g., rice) might be more complex. As for Lipton's explanation of the "price twists" by reference to the "urban bias" of policymakers, it does not seem to be entirely satisfactory, for it fails to take into account the specific economic and political determinants of this phenomenon.

A structural-economic explanation of low agricultural prices in industrializing dependent societies is developed by de Janvry (1981). According to him, in these societies industrialization takes place without a considerable expansion of domestic markets, which perpetuates low urban and rural wages and low food prices. The same argument can be applied to the prices of domestically produced industrial inputs — cotton, in this case. This explanation, however, focuses entirely on the structural-economic determinants of state policies, leaving no room for analysing dynamic political factors which might influence their formulation. In Peru, for example, the policy of low cotton prices was pursued not only during the period of import-substitution industrialization under the Velasco regime, but also after the demise of military populism, when industrialization had lost its original momentum. It could be explained, in part, by the government's support for industrial exports, characteristic of the period of transition to economic neoliberalism in Peru. No less important, however, was the political pressure exercised by textile industrialists whose interests were defended by the powerful Industrial Society. Their influence clearly outweighed the influence of the co-operativized cotton producers, as represented by the CNA.

The role of organized pressure from social and political actors was even more obvious in the implementation of agricultural policies. The problem of co-operative agricultural wages provides a good example. Even though cotton co-operatives were rather unsuccessful in influencing government price policies, they obtained considerable wage concessions. As already noted, real agricultural wages in the state-sponsored co-operatives studied tended to grow despite the Morales government's policy of wage controls. In fact, it was precisely the combination of the cotton producers' failure to obtain higher cotton prices and their success in obtaining higher co-operative wages (and other benefits) that contributed, significantly, to the crisis in the cotton co-operative economy.

These considerations raise doubts about the validity of de Janvry's causal chain leading from dependent industrialization to low urban wages, low agricultural prices, and eventually to low rural wages. This chain may appear as a general tendency, reflecting the structural peculiarities of dependent economies. However, it can be broken by the organized pressure of social and political actors, as occurred with co-operativized cotton producers in Peru.

The importance of political factors can also be seen in agricultural credit policies, although in this case they are more closely related to the government's political orientations. Velasco's military-populist government offered the co-operative sector cheap, abundant short-term credit in a clear attempt to facilitate its development in opposition to private agriculture. De Janvry admits that low agricultural prices in industrializing dependent economies can be combined with state support for commercial (in Peru's case, co-operative) agriculture, a support which he feels is designed to relieve pressure on the national balance of payments. In the Velasco regime, however, this support reflected not so much the government's concern with the balance of payments, as its commitment to a radical populist and developmentalist ideology emphasizing popular consumption and co-operation. This commitment made the Velasco government pursue promotional credit policies which went beyond agricultural production objectives and which, economically, clearly contradicted the policies of agricultural price controls.

De Janvry's structural determinism finds an analytical counterpart in O'Donnell's conception of political change. While de Janvry explains economic policies by reference to economic structures, O'Donnell views political organization through economic policies which reflect predominant social alliances. According to O'Donnell (1979), the development of post-populist alliance between the state bureaucracy, transnational capital, and segments of the national bourgeoisie economically and politically excludes the popular sectors forming part of the populist coalition. This exclusion is manifested in the establishment of authoritarian-bureaucratic regimes adopting anti-popular economic policies (involving, in Peru's case, a shift toward economic neo-liberalism). This conception is criticized by Cardoso (1970) and Kaufman (1979) who point to the absence of a one-on-one link between socio-economic and political transformation. Their argument is confirmed by the Peruvian experience, which demonstrates that post-populist transition to economic neo-liberalism can take place within authoritarian and liberal-democratic political frameworks alike.

It should also be noted that the actual outcomes of political transformation triggered by a change in the predominant social alliances are determined not only by governments' attempts to modify national political organization in accordance with the interests of the dominant classes (as O'Donnell seems to believe), but also by popular political responses to these attempts. An excessive focus on government policies, however, can substitute the analysis of policy for that of actual political practices. This fallacy can be seen in the discussion of Peruvian corporatism under the Velasco regime developed by Stepan (1978), for instance. Stepan concentrates almost exclusively on government corporatist ideology and policy. However, as the early experiences of the post-reform co-operative movement indicate, the state-sponsored popular organizations did not always follow the corporatist rules of the game established for them by the state. This, in turn, imposed severe limitations on the actual implementation of the government's corporatist project.

The role of popular organizations in determining political outcomes became even more important during the rule of Morales, who attempted to combine orthodox economic policymaking with a policy politically excluding the popular sectors. These attempts resulted in a popular political mobilization against his regime, effectively contributing to the return of liberal democracy and to the political inclusion of the popular sectors under Belaunde. The political success of popular organizations, however, did not imply a success in economic policies. The democratically elected government of Belaunde continued the transition to economic neo-liberalism started by Morales. In other words, the political inclusion of the popular sectors was not followed by their economic inclusion (at least during the Belaunde administration). This can be explained by the relatively low effectiveness of popular political pressure on economic policies, which, in the case at hand, was exemplified by the controversial experience of the CNA-led co-operative mobilization.

At least two sets of factors seemed to be responsible for this relatively low effectiveness. One set of factors was related to the difficulties involved in forming political alliances between organizations representing popular sectors with different economic interests. The CNA's failure to forge a joint agrarian opposition can be largely explained by the diverging interests of its own social base (agricultural co-operatives) and those of community peasants, as represented by the CCP. Political differences between these two organizations also played a role in this failure. More important, however, was the impossibility of accommodating the concerns of the land-hungry peasants with the co-operatives' demands for higher state-controlled agricultural prices and lower Agrarian Bank interest rates.

The second set of factors was related to the internal problems of the popular political bodies. The CNA had difficulties in forming an alliance with the CCP and in mobilizing its own membership. This second difficulty could be attributed to factors such as the bureaucratic origin of the CNA, which impeded communication between the leaders and most of the membership, and the selective repression used by the Belaunde government against co-operative leaders. More fundamentally, however, the difficulties reflected the eternal dilemma presented to social actors facing policy-related problems — the dilemma between political and non-political courses of action. The economic crisis at the root of the co-operative political mobilization was caused primarily by government economic policies. Nevertheless, the non-political solutions to the crisis, such as internal reorganization and subdivision, appeared to many co-operative members as less costly and generally more attractive than the political mobilization advocated by the CNA. As a consequence, only a part of the co-operative membership supported mobilization, while an increasing number of co-operatives opted for subdivision.

The organizational weakness of popular political bodies and the difficulties in co-ordinating their activities can be responsible for the low effectiveness of popular participation under liberal-democratic regimes and may make these regimes politically exclusionary in fact if not in law.

Appendices

Appendix 1

ORGANIZATION CHART, CAP ALAMOS

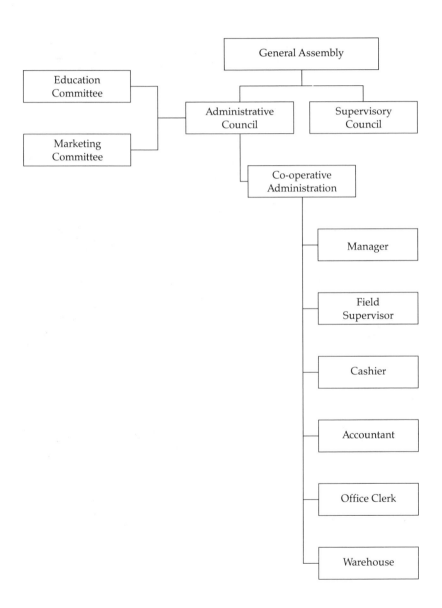

Appendix 2

ORGANIZATION CHART, CAP SIGLO XX

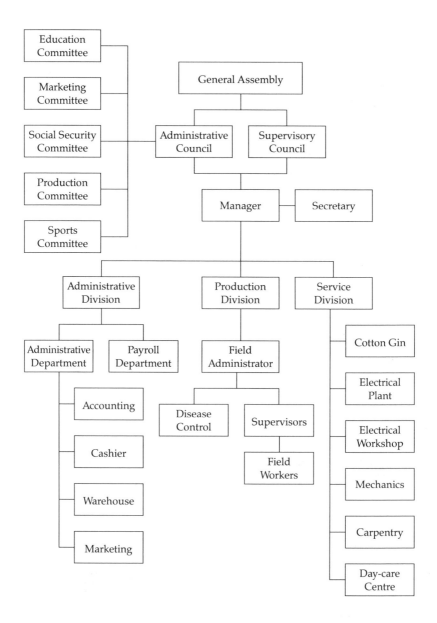

Appendix 3

ORGANIZATION CHART, CAP MONTE BLANCO

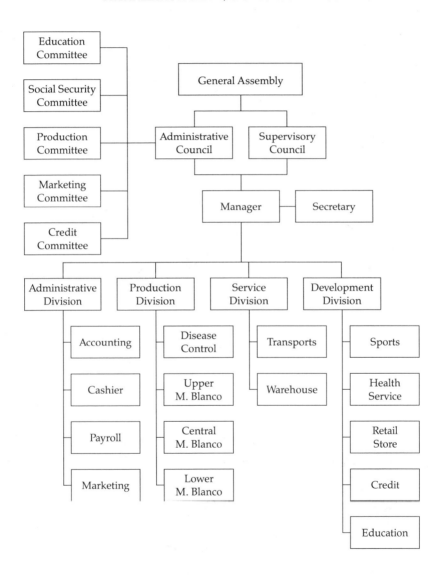

Appendix 4

Cotton yields and Structure of Cotton Production Costs per Hectare (Tanguis variety, *planta*) in Co-operatives and Valley Studied

Items	Alamos	Siglo xx	Monte Blanco	Valley Average
YIELDS (in q.)	52	55	51	45
STRUCTURE OF PRODUCTION COSTS				
Labour force (person-hours)				
Soil preparation	6	7	9	7
Sowing and fertilizing	3	3	2	2
Cultivation (weeding, irrigation, etc.)	33	43	38	37
Disease control	1	3	1	1
Harvesting	40	36	34	37
Total	83	92	84	84
Mechanical traction (tractor-hours)				
Soil preparation	10	12	12	12
Sowing and fertilizing	3	2	2	2
Cultivation (weeding, irrigation, etc.)	8	7	8	8
Disease control	1	2	2	2
Harvesting	—	2	—	—
Total	22	25	24	24
Inputs				
Seed (q.)	1.5	1.5	1.5	1.5
Fertilizers (kg)				
urea	300	228	250	350
ammonium phosphate	—	130	150	150
superphosphate	400	—	—	—
Pesticides				
pentachlorine (kg)	0.5	—	0.5	1
demonsan (lb)	—	1	—	0.5
endrin (lb)	3	1.5	1.5	3
lead arsenate (lb)	16	16	25	25
calcium arsenate (lb)	10	20	20	20
metasystox (l)	0.15	0.5	0.25	0.3
Water (in thousand m³)				
subterranean	10	13	9	13
superficial	—	—	3	

SOURCES: Co-operative production plans (Alamos 1979–80; Siglo xx 1983–4; Monte Blanco 1977–8); Cotton Production Committee, Departmental Office, 1979–80

Notes

CHAPTER ONE: INTRODUCTION

1 See, for example, UNRISD (1969, 1971, 1975). For a discussion of co-operative principles, see ICA (1976) and Craig and Saxena (1984).

2 For a general analysis of Latin American agrarian structures, see Stavenhagen (1975), Furtado (1976), and Pearse (1975). The persistence of precapitalist labour relations under market economy conditions in Latin America is discussed by Laclau (1979).

3 For an analysis of the capitalist transformation of agriculture in Latin America, see Goodman and Redclift (1981), and Feder (1980). For a review of Latin American literature on the subject, see Harris (1978). On the growth of small capitalist production in some areas of Latin America, see Murmis (1981) and Llambi (1988).

4 For a general discussion of land reforms in Latin America, see García (1973), Furtado (1976), Lehmann (1978), de Janvry and Ground (1978), and Grindle (1986).

5 The same argument was developed by de Janvry in his later works. See de Janvry (1981, 1984).

6 For a detailed discussion of the relation between land reform and rural poverty in Latin America, see Grindle (1986). In the case of Peru, see Alberts (1983).

7 Similar observations are frequently made about rural development projects in general. It has been repeatedly argued that governments' attempts to implement these projects tend to consolidate old and create new social inequalities, as well as to establish vertical controls over the rural population. See Galli (1981), Wolfe (1984), Lele (1981), and Cohen and Uphoff (1980).

8 This view was developed with particular cogency by supporters of the "structuralist" school; see Feder (1971), Barraclough and Domike (1970), and

159

Barraclough (1973). For a general analysis of the performance of Latin American agriculture, see Barraclough (1977, 1981), García (1981), and de Janvry (1981).

9 According to Lipton (1977), in less developed countries the capital/output ratios for agriculture are higher than they are in industry. For an analysis of the urban character of the European intellectual tradition in Latin America, see Burns (1982).

10 For a critique of Lipton's approach, see Corbridge (1982), Byres (1977), and Redclift (1984).

11 For an alternative approach emphasizing the importance of political and ideological factors, see Lefeber and North (1980) and Grindle (1986).

12 See, for example, the collections of articles edited by Malloy (1979), Collier (1979), and O'Brien and Cammack (1985).

13 For a discussion of corporatism in Latin America, see, in addition to Wiarda, Pike and Stritch (1974) and Malloy (1979).

14 Stepan's definition of corporatism is close to the one offered by Schmitter (1974), who compares Latin American corporatism to corporatism in Western industrial societies.

15 This line of analysis is developed in the dependency perspective by Evans (1979) and Gereffi (1983).

16 It is not my intention here to engage in a detailed discussion of the concept of bureaucratic authoritarianism. The reader interested in the subject should refer to Remmer and Merkx (1982), Epstein (1984), Canak (1984), Wallerstein (1980), Carnoy (1984), Collier (1979), and Cammack (1985) among others.

17 These arguments were developed by Hirschman (1979), Serra (1979), and Foxley (1979). See also Furtad (1987), Thorp and Whitehead (1982).

18 See, for example, Cardoso (1979), Kaufman (1979), and Sheahan (1980).

19 First published in 1969, this study is now considered a classic text on dependency theory. Because of its focus on national structures and processes, as well as the importance attributed to social and political actors, it largely escaped the harsh criticisms directed at dependency theory. For a discussion of Cardoso and Faletto's work, see Cammack (1985), Blomström and Hettne (1984), and Carnoy (1984). See also Cardoso (1973, 1977, 1979).

CHAPTER TWO: AGRICULTURAL CO-OPERATIVES UNDER MILITARY POPULISM, 1969-75

1 According to Wolf's and Mintz's typology, the capitalist estates would fall under the category of plantations rather than haciendas (Wolf and Mintz 1977). In Peru, however, the term hacienda is used with reference to all large estates, regardless of their organization.

2 The system of peonage (*colonato*) was based on the use of bond labour. It was

practiced largely on coastal rice estates and on highland livestock haciendas. Sharecropping was more typical of cotton estates on the coast (*yanaconaje*) and crop or crop-livestock haciendas in the highlands (*aparceria*) (Kay 1982:142-3; Montoya 1978; Paige 1975).

3 Montoya (1978:Appendix, Table 1). The remaining 17 per cent fall under the category of family labour, the bulk of which was probably occupied in the smallholding sector. See also Montoya (1979) and Matos Mar and Mejía (1980;42).

4 For a detailed analysis of this process, see Matos Mar (1976). Thorp and Bertram mention that another factor contributing to the decline of sharecropping was the introduction of a credit system which gave preference to large cotton producers involved in direct cultivation (Thorp and Bertram 1978:174-5).

5 For a discussion of seasonal migration in Peru, see Caballero (1981). On the importance of wage earning in the highland peasant economy, see Figueroa (1977, 1980, 1982).

6 For a discussion of the 1969 land reform in Peru, see Matos Mar and Mejía (1980), Kay (1982), Caballero (1977), Valderrama (1982), North (1981), Zaldívar (1974), Strasma (1976), Montoya (1979), Collin Delavaud (1980), and Alberts (1983).

7 The methodology used for converting regular into standardized hectares is discussed by Caballero and Alvarez (1980, Appendix 1).

8 In 1969, the government introduced modifications in Decree-Law 17716, prohibiting the subdivision of estates by private initiative. In 1971, it reversed the court decision on the subdivision of the hacienda Huando and transformed it into a production co-operative, despite the protests of medium producers.

9 For a description of co-operative organization in Peru, see Martínez (1980) and IPEC (1982).

10 State controls over cotton co-operatives were, however, less stringent than for the sugar co-operative sector, supervised by a special government agency, SAF-CAP (Horton 1976:188-9; García-Sayán 1977:146-8). See also Cleaves and Scurrah (1980) and McClintock (1982, 1983).

11 For an analysis of industrial policies under Velasco, see Portocarrero (1981), González (1981), and Garaycochea (1981).

12 A distinction should be made here between traditional and non-traditional exports. Non-traditional exports, including, most importantly, the exports of manufactured goods, received government subsidies. Cotton, however, belonged to the category of traditional exports, which did not enjoy this support.

13 On the development of the textile industry in Peru, see Fernández-Baca and Tume (1981).

14 The expansion of the state-controlled sector is generally considered to be one

of the most important characteristics of the Velasco regime. On the role of the state in the Peruvian economy, see Fitzgerald (1979, 1983).

15 Cotton producers were paid in accordance with the floor prices (*precio basico*), after they handed over their produce to cotton gins or EPCHAP agencies. After the cotton fibre was sold on the international market, they received an additional lump payment (*reintegro*). In 1975, it was approximately 16 per cent of the initial payment.

16 On the role of food imports in the Peruvian economy, see Lajo (1981, 1982).

17 For an analysis of the causes of the economic crisis, see Thorp (1979, 1983), Schydlowsky and Wicht (1983), and Fitzgerald (1983), among others.

18 In the Chancay Valley, the transfer of haciendas to their workers was completed only four years after land reform began, under strong pressure from local unions (Mejía and Díaz 1975:120). In the Huaral and Cañete Valleys, the unions mobilized their members against the division of haciendas by their owners. Piura probably was the most interesting case where the beginning of land reform triggered land invasions and strikes conducted not only by hacienda unions, but also by local smallholders and temporary labourers (García-Sayán 1982:24-9).

19 The CCP was founded in 1956 by the Communist party. By the late 1960s, it had come under the control of Maoist groups and concentrated its activities in the highlands, supporting peasant struggles against haciendas.

20 In this sense, the situation of cotton co-operatives differed considerably from that of the sugar sector. The sugar labour unions had a much longer experience of political struggles. At the same time, after land reform, they confronted more rigorous state controls than those imposed on cotton co-operatives. As a consequence, the co-operativization of sugar haciendas produced an open confrontation between the unions and the state, culminating in strikes (Pease 1977a; Valderrama 1976).

21 The most famous case was that of Andahuaylas. In 1974, this highland province saw a massive invasion of co-operative lands by peasant communities. According to some estimates, the invasions involved around thirty thousand peasants and affected sixty-six estates, most of them co-operative property. See Sánchez (1981) and García-Sayán (1982, Ch. 2).

22 In addition to Stepan (1979), see Cotler (1972, 1975), Palmer (1973), Palmer and Middlebrook (1976), Santistevan (1977), Collier (1975, 1976).

23 According to Matos Mar and Mejía (1980, Table 51), the proportion of co-operative workers in the CNA's total membership was even lower — 10 per cent.

CHAPTER THREE: CO-OPERATIVES IN THE POST-POPULIST CONTEXT, 1975-83

1 For an analysis of the stabilization programs conducted by the Morales

government, see Thorp (1983), Schydlowsky and Wicht (1983), and Stallings (1983).

2 For a general analysis of post-populist economic neo-liberalism in Peru, see Pease (1981b) and Portocarrero (1980, Ch. 5).

3 According to Revesz, in the second half of the 1970s, the average prices of cotton for textile industries in Peru were between 30 and 50 per cent lower than the average international prices (Revesz 1982:406).

4 The relatively favourable situation in the rice-growing sector reflected the persistence of the government's concern with domestic rice production, even after it had generally abandoned promotional policies for food crops. This concern could probably be explained by the overwhelming importance of rice in the Peruvian urban diet. Moreover, most rice production came from private farms, which, according to the prevailing neo-liberal views, constituted the backbone of national agriculture and therefore deserved state support.

5 For an analysis of the development of the jungle area, see Ballon (1982) and Ponce (1982).

6 The implications of the Agrarian Promotion Law for national agriculture in general and the co-operative sector in particular are discussed by Mejía (1980), Revesz (1980), Barrenechea and Valcarcel (1981), McClintock (1982) and CEPES (1981a).

7 De facto, the restructuring started long before the passing of the Law. In 1977, the government intervened and restructured eleven out of eighteen agricultural co-operatives in Alto Piura. The co-operatives had failed to repay their loans to the Agrarian Bank, owing to financial difficulties aggravated in this area by a drought. In addition, they had to reduce their agricultural area and, in some cases, to suspend paying wages to their members who, in compensation, had been granted access to the co-operative lands on an individual basis. The co-operative lands also had been invaded by local smallholders excluded from land reform.

After the government intervention, the co-operatives were forced to adopt austerity measures, which enabled them to pay their debts to the Bank. At the same time, the government implemented a sweeping reorganization program, transferring most of the co-operative lands to the individual ownership of both the former co-operative members and the local smallholders. According to the data of the Ministry of Agriculture, by 1980, approximately 70 per cent of the co-operative lands in the area had been privatized in this way (cited in Castillo 1980:81).

8 On the evolution of the labour movement in Peru, see Scurrah and Esteves (1982), Dietz (1982), and Sulmont (1978, 1981), in addition to Pease (1981a).

9 The strike followed the announcement of a new stabilization program which, in some estimates, would have resulted in an 18 per cent decrease in real wages (Pease 1981a:300). The strikers' demands included the suspen-

sion of the announced stabilization measures, labour stability and wage increases, as well as better credit facilities and higher farm prices for agricultural producers.

10 The transition itself may be partly explained by the resistance of the popular organizations to the Morales regime. Pease (1981a), however, suggests that more important in this sense was the continuing pressure for political, and further economic, liberalization, coming from domestic entrepreneurs. Even if they welcomed Morales' exclusionary policies toward popular organizations, they still saw their interests threatened by the persistence of state controls over the national economy. The Morales government had considerably relaxed these controls, in accordance with orthodox economic strategies. However, the military were reluctant to dismantle the state economic sector, seeing in it the main source of their political autonomy vis-à-vis powerful private interests. Confronted with growing opposition from both the popular sectors and the national bourgeoisie, the military opted for withdrawl from politics. The general presidential and parliamentary elections held in 1980 gave power to the Popular Action party closely related to business circles and committed to further liberalization of the national economy. For an analysis of the electoral process and of the platforms of major political parties, see Bernales (1980), and Woy-Hazleton (1982). See also Pease (1981b) and Cotler (1980).

11 For an analysis of the CNA's position on agricultural and land policies, see CNA (1979, 1980, 1981, 1982a).

12 For the CCP's position on these issues, see CCP (1980, 1981, 1982, 1983).

13 Significantly, FRADEPT was affiliated with both agrarian confederations, the CNA and the CCP. FRADEPT had been created during the Velasco administration as part of the CNA organizational network. Later, however, it incorporated the Catacaos community — an influential member of the CCP — and became affiliated with the CCP. FRADEPT persistently advocated the merger of the CNA and CCP. This proposition was also supported by the CCP national leadership but opposed by the CNA, which insisted on preserving the organizational autonomy of each of the two confederations.

14 It also included a demand to abolish the Anti-Terrorist Law, directed presumably against the guerrillas conducted by the Maoist "Shining Path," but used extensively for the persecution of CCP and CNA leaders. Reports on the strike are provided by the CNA (1982b), among others.

15 Excellent reports on the social and economic situation in the co-operative sector are provided by CEPES (1981a,b,c).

CHAPTER FOUR: THE ORIGIN AND SOCIO-ECONOMIC ORGANIZATION OF THE COTTON CO-OPERATIVES

1 According to the data of the Departmental Office of the Ministry of Agricul-

ture, the level of subterranean waters in the valley fell from 20 m in 1965 to 90 m in 1979. At the turn of the decade, the valley had an acute shortage of water for irrigation.

2 The average land per capita ratio in the area of the valley affected by land reform was 3.4 ha, while according to the Ministry of Agriculture the minimum size of a viable family farm on the coast was 4 ha.

3 Some of these programs tended to benefit those who were already well-off. Thus, personal loans to employees came to double and triple loans granted to manual workers. The members who benefitted most from the housing program were those who already had some personal savings. As for work clothes, manual workers were handed ordinary overalls, while employees received business suits ("like those they wear in the bank"), a fact which was frequently recalled with intense resentment by the manual workers interviewed. In addition, the implementation of the projects was accompanied by a huge financial scandal, implicating the president of the Administrative Council and some senior employees.

4 Even this measure, however, could not be easily implemented. One overseer, for instance, refused to move to another sector and continued to attend to his duties, along with the new supervisor appointed by the administration. Whoever came first to the field in the morning distributed tasks among the workers who obeyed both, but jeeringly. Finally, the administration backed down and removed the new overseer from the controversial sector.

5 The number of privately owned livestock grew steadily throughout the 1970s. In 1981, one of the three co-operative field sectors, comprising sixty-five field worker families, owned between seventy and eighty heads of beef and milk cattle in addition to 300 sheep and goats.

CHAPTER FIVE: CO-OPERATIVE
INSTITUTIONS: INTERNAL PARTICIPATION
AND EXTERNAL POLITICAL INVOLVEMENT

1 Alamos took part in almost all regional and some national training programs for co-operative members. In 1971, it sent members to a seminar on business administration and agricultural technology by CENCIRA; in 1972, to a program in accounting offered by ONDECOOP. In 1976 and 1978, once again, some members took courses in administration, technology, and social development offered by the Ministry of Agriculture, SINAMOS, the Agrarian Bank, and the Ministry of Health. When, in 1976, the National Central Co-operative (CENASCONTEC) was formed with the objective of supervising co-operative accounting, the bookkeeper from Alamos became its first president. Subsequently, Alamos participated in two or three seminars in accounting offered by this organization.

2 This field worker became the most prominent figure in the co-operative epic.

The account of his one-year presidency is particularly interesting because it sheds light not only on the experience of worker participation in management in a large state-sponsored co-operative, but also on the complexities of co-operative and regional alliances.

Before the land reform, the person in question (I will call him Sanchez) had been a trade union leader. After the co-operativization of the hacienda, he was elected as the secretary-general of the co-operative union. He also held several low-ranking positions on the co-operative councils. His election as the president of the Administrative Council in 1978 ended the first five-year period of the employees' rule and represented an important, even though not lasting, victory of the co-operative field workers.

As president, Sanchez pursued two mutually complementary strategies: first, he invested heavily in co-operative economic and social infrastructure and second, he started a war against corruption. During his presidency, the co-operative purchased four trucks, four tractors, various types of agricultural equipment and a number of milk cows (which somehow turned out to be beef cattle and which disappeared soon after Sanchez left the presidency). The co-operative also started building a new civic centre, apparently without the permission of the municipal authorities.

At the same time, Sanchez made an attempt to break the power of the co-operative "mafia." He fired the co-operative manager, increased his own administrative powers, promoted his supporters (mostly younger manual workers) to employees positions, and imposed rigorous controls on both factory transactions and labour discipline in the field.

While the actual impact of these measures on the co-operative economy is hard to evaluate, their social implications were disastrous. The employees accused Sanchez of embezzling funds and took the case to court. Curiously, the accusation struck a positive response among his own supporters. Sanchez's administrative ascendancy, his intransigence with even minor infractions of labour discipline and the promotion of his political allies were bitterly resented by his former fellow field workers.

Sanchez managed to turn against himself not only almost the entire membership, but also the bureaucrats entrenched in the local offices of the Ministry of Agriculture and the related administrative bodies, many of whom had benefitted from close relationships with the co-operative "mafia." In 1978, Sanchez was elected president of the Central Co-operative and, in this capacity, he tracked down some of the financial irregularities committed after land reform by the manager of the regional Special Committee (who, after this scandal, had to resign his position in the Ministry of Agriculture and turned to melon marketing through agreements with the co-operatives, an arrangement which left many of them with heavy losses).

By contrast, SINAMOS and the CNA, whose representatives were frequently involved in confrontations with local bureaucrats from the Ministry of Agriculture, supported Sanchez's initiatives. This support, however, was moderated by their fear of alienating the established co-operative leadership against whom Sanchez had rebelled.

The net outcome of this complicated political game, which developed simultaneously at the co-operative and the regional levels, was the expulsion of Sanchez from the co-operative, followed by his one-year imprisonment and a long series of trials which ended in 1982 with his exoneration. Despite his repeated requests, however, he was never readmitted to the co-operative.

CHAPTER SIX: CO-OPERATIVE ECONOMY IN CRISIS

1 As indicated in Chapter 5, local agriculture was heavily dependent on the deposits of subterranean water gradually diminishing as a result of overexploitation. The radical solution to the problem would have been, of course, to tap the unused water resources in the adjacent highland regions. The implementation of such a project, however, was far beyond the financial capacity of local producers. A partial, less expensive solution would have been the substitution of less demanding perennial crops, such as grapes or fruit trees, for the water-consuming crops with a short vegetable cycle, including cotton. However, even this change would have required investments beyond the means of local producers. Alamos was one of the few co-operatives in the valley which made a deliberate effort to expand the planting of perennial crops.

2 According to the Irrigation Department of the Regional Ministry of Agriculture, in 1982 the operating costs of the oil pumps were almost five times higher than those of the electrical ones.

3 The advantage, though, turned out to be rather dubious. For some obscure reason, ELECTROPERU charged the co-operative not the relatively low agricultural or agro-industrial rates but a much higher industrial one. The difference became critical in the 1980s, when the co-operative found itself unable to pay its electricity bills. In 1982, it owed ELECTROPERU 136 million *soles*, a considerable sum even for an entreprise as big as Siglo XX. To add to the co-operative's misfortunes, its electric transformer broke down, leaving half of the irrigation wells out of order. The repair work took several months, during which time the co-operative's crops did not receive the required water.

4 Siglo XX spent part of its net earnings on the agrarian debt (20 million *soles* per year until 1977) and, from 1978 onward, on income tax. Between 20 and 30 per cent of the earnings were invested in agricultural machinery and equipment. The remainder was split between co-operative funds and individual payments.

5 Monte Blanco's net earnings (left over after deducting total administrative expenses from sales revenues) were spent more or less in the same fashion as

at Siglo XX. The co-operative had to pay its agrarian debt (160 thousand *soles* per year until 1977) and, from 1978 onwards, income tax. Around 20 per cent of the earnings were reinvested, mostly in the purchase of agricultural machinery and equipment. The remaining profits were partly used for co-operative needs and partly distributed among co-operative members.

Bibliography

Alberts, Tom. 1983. *Agrarian Reform and Rural Poverty: A Case Study of Peru*. Boulder CO: Westview Press

Alvarez, Elena. 1980. *Política agraria y estancamiento de la agricultura. 1969-1977*. Lima: IEP (Instituto de Estudios Peruanos)

Ballon, Francisco. 1982. "La nueva conquista de la Amazonia," in *Promoción agraria: ¿ Para quién?*, José M. Meíja, ed., pp. 63-83. Lima: Tiempo Presente

Baretta, Silvio D., and Helen E. Douglass. 1977. "Authoritarianism and Corporatism in Latin America: A Review Essay," in *Authoritarianism and Corporatism in Latin America*, James Malloy, ed., 513-24. Pittsburgh: University of Pittsburgh Press

Barraclough, Solon L. 1973. *Agrarian Structure in Latin America*. Lexington KY: D.C. Health

— 1977. "Agricultural Production Prospects in Latin America," *World Development*, 5 (5-7):459-76

— 1981. "Perspectivas de la crisis agrícola en la América Latina," in *Desarrollo agrario y la América Latina*, Antonio Garcia, ed., pp. 395-428. Mexico City: Fondo de Cultura Económica

Barraclough, Solon L., and Arthur Domike. 1970. "Agrarian Structure in Seven Latin American Countries," in *Agrarian Structure and Peasant Movements in Latin America*, Rodolfo Stavenhagen, ed., pp. 41-94. New York: Doubleday

Barrenechea, Carlos, and Marcel Valcárcel. 1981. *Situación del agro nacional y significado de la Ley de la Promoción y Desarrollo*. Lima: Universidad Agraria La Molina. Mimeo

BCR (Banco Central de Reserva). 1980a. *Reseña económica*

— 1980b. *Memoria 1980*

— 1982a. *Reseña económica*

— 1982b. *Memoria 1982*

— 1983. *Memoria 1983*

Bernales, Enrique. 1980. *Crisis política: solución electoral?* Lima: DESCO (Centro de Estudios y Promoción del Dessarrollo)

Billone, Jorge, et al. 1982. *Términos de intercambio ciudad-campo 1970-1980: precios y excedente agrario.* Lima: CEDEP (Centro de Estudios para el Dessarrollo y la Participación)

Blomström, Magnus, and Hettne, Björn 1984. *Development Theory in Transition: The Dependency Debate and Beyond: Third World Responses.* London: Zed Books

Burns, Bradford E. 1982. *The Poverty of Progress: Latin America in the Nineteenth Century.* Berkeley CA: University of California Press

Byres, T.J. 1977. "Agrarian Transition and the Agrarian Question," *The Journal of Peasant Studies*, 4. April: 258-74

Caballero, José María. 1977. "Sobre el carácter de la Reforma Agraria," in *Latin American Perspectives* 4 (3):146-59

— 1980. "El fracaso del modelo agrario del régimen militar," in *Realidad del campo peruano despues de la Reforma Agraria*, 67-104. Lima: CIC (Centro de Investigación y Capacitación)

— 1981. *Economia agraria de la Sierra peruana (autes de la Reforma Agraria de 1969).* Lima: IEP (Instituto de Estudios Peruanos)

— 1984. "Agriculture and the Peasantry under Industrialization Pressure: Lessons from the Peruvian Experience," in *Latin American Research Review*, 19 (2):3-41

Caballero, Jose Maria, and Elena Alvarez. 1980. *Aspectos quantitativos de la Reforma Agraria.* Lima: IEP (Instituto de Estudios Peruanos)

Cammack, Paul 1985. "The Political Economy of Contemporary Military Regimes in Latin America: From Bureaucratic Authoritarianism to Restructuring," in *Generals in Retreat: The Crisis of the Military Rule*, Philip O'Brien and Paul Cammack, eds., pp. 1-36, Manchester: Manchester University Press

Canak, William L. 1984. "The Peripheral State Debate: State Capitalist and Bureaucratic Authoritarian Regimes in Latin America," *Latin American Research Review* 19 (1):3-36

Cardoso, Fernando H. 1973. "Associated Dependent Development: Theoretical and Practical Implications," *Authoritarian Brazil: Origins, Policies and Future*, New Haven and London: Yale University Press

Cardoso, Fernando H. 1977. "The Consumption of Dependency Theory in the United States," *Latin American Research Review* 12 (3)

Cardoso, Fernando H. 1979. "On the Characterization of Authoritarian Regimes in Latin America," in *The New Authoritarianism in Latin America*, David Collier, ed., 33-57. Princeton: Princeton University Press

Cardoso, Fernando H., and Enzo Faletto. 1979. *Dependency and Development in Latin America*. Berkeley CA: University of California Press

Carnoy, Martin 1984. *The State and Political Theory*. Princeton: Princeton University Press

Castillo, Hernán. 1980. "La restructuración de la tenencia de la tierra y de las empresas asociativas," in *Promoción agraria: ¿ Para quién?*, Jose M. Mejía, ed., pp. 84-104. Lima: Tiempo Presente

CCP (Confederación Campesina del Perú). 1980. *Posición de la CCP frente a la Ley de la Promoción y Desarrollo Agrario*. Lima: CCP

— 1981a. *Segundo Consejo Nacional CCP: Informes y Resoluciones, 20-22 de febrero. Comunidad de San Pedro de Casta*. Lima: CCP, Secretaría de Prensa y Propaganda

— 1981b. *Informativo legal agrario: Las cooperativas agrarias de producción de la Costa y las parcelaciones*. Special Report

— 1982. *Cuarto Consejo Nacional de la CCP: Acuerdos y Resoluciones. Comunidad de Santa Rosa de Melgar. Puno. 29-31 enero*. Lima: CCP, Secretaría de Prensa y Propaganda

— 1983. *Programa Agrario (Acuerdos del Sexto Congreso)*. Lima: CCP, Escuelas Campesinas

CEPES (Centro de Promoción y Estudios Sociales). 1981a. *Informativo legal agrario: Reglamento de Promoción y Desarrollo Agrario*. Special Report

— 1981. *Informativo legal agrario: La nueva Ley de Cooperativas y el agro*. (June-July)

Cleaves, Peter S., and Martin J. Scurrah. 1980. *Agriculture, Bureaucracy, and Military Government in Peru*. Ithaca NY: Cornell University Press

CNA (Confederación Nacional Agraria). 1975. *Estatuto de la Confederación Nacional Agraria*. Lima: CNA, Departamento de la Prensa y Difusion, Mimeo

— 1977. *La CNA y la Asamblea Constituyente*. Lima: CNA. Mimeo

— 1979. *Acuerdos y conclusiones: Segundo Congreso Nacional Agrario, CAP La Achirana, Ica*. Lima: CNA, Secretaría de la Prensa y Difusion

— 1980. *Septima Asamblea Nacional de delegados de la CNA: Acuerdos y conclusiones, 18-20 diciembre de 1980. Eaños del Inca. Cajamarca*. Lima: Ediciones Tierra

— 1981. *Hacia una alternativa agraria: Foro organizado por la Confederación Nacional Agraria*. Lima: CNA, Secretaría de La Prensay Difusión

— 1982a. *Acuerdos y conclusiones: Tercer Congreso Nacional. Santa Rosa de Ocopa, 21-24 junio, 1982*. Lima: CNA, Secretaría de la Prensay Difusión

— 1982b. *Tierra: Informativo de la Confederación Nacional Agraria*. Special Issue (December)

Cohen, John M., and Uphoff, Norman T. 1980. "Participation's Place in Rural Development: Seeking Clarity through Specificity," *World Development* 8:213-35

Collin Delavaud, Claude. 1967. "Consequencia de la modernización de la agricultura en las haciendas de la Costa Norte del Perú," in *Hacienda, comunidad y campesinado en el Perú*, José Matos Mar, ed., pp. 139-75. Lima: IEP (Instituto de Estudios Peruanos)

— 1980. "Agrarian Reform in Peru," in *Environment, Society and Rural Change in Latin America*, David A. Preston, ed., pp. 37-52. Chichester UK: John Wiley

Collier, David. 1976. "The Politics of Squatter Settlement Formation in Peru," in *Peruvian Nationalism: A Corporatist Revolution*, David Chaplin, ed., 173-204. New Brunswick: Transaction Books

— 1979. "Overview of the Bureaucratic-Authoritarian Model," in *The New Authoritarianism in Latin America*, David Collier, ed., 19-32. Princeton: Princeton University Press

Corbridge, Stuart. 1982. "Urban Bias, Rural Bias and Industrialization: An Appraisal of the Work of Michael Lipton and Terry Byres," in *Rural Development: Theory of Peasant Economy and Agrarian Change*, John Harriss, ed., pp. 94-116. London: Hutchinson University Library

Cotler, Julio. 1972. "Bases del corporativismo en el Perú," in *Sociedad y Política*, pp. 4-25

— 1975. "The New Mode of Political Domination in Peru," in *The Peruvian Experiment: Continuity and Change Under Military Rule*, Abraham F. Lowerthal, ed., pp. 44-78, Princeton: Princeton University Press

— 1980. *Democracia e integración nacional*. Lima: IEP (Instituto de Estudios Peruanos)

Cotler, Julio, and Felipe Portocarrero. 1969. "Peru: Peasant Organization," in *Latin American Peasant Movements*, Henry A. Landsberger, ed., pp. 297-322, Ithaca NY: Cornell University Press

Craig, J.G., and S.K. Saxena. 1984. "A Critical Assessment of the Co-operative Principles," Paper presented to the 4th Symposium on Participatory Development Through Community-Cooperative Interaction, Tel Aviv, Israel, 9 April

Dietz, Henry A. 1982. "Mobilization, Austerity and Voting: The Legacy of the Revolution for Lima's Poor," in *Post-Revolutionary Peru: The Politics of Transformation*, Stephen M. Gorman ed., pp. 73-99. Boulder CO: Westview Press

di Tella, Torcuato. 1970. "Populism and Reform in Latin America," in *Obstacles to Change in Latin America*, Claudio Veliz, ed., pp. 47-75. New York: Oxford University Press

Eguren, Fernando. 1977. "Politíca agraria y estructura agraria," in *Estado y política agraria*. Lima: DESCO (Centro de Estudios y Promoción del Desarrollo)

— 1981. "Evolución de la producción algodonera," in *Producción algodonera e industria textil en el Perú*, Fernando Eguren, et al., pp. 11-125. Lima: DESCO (Centro de Estudios y Promoción del Desarrollo)

Epstein, Edward 1984. "Legitimacy, Institutionalization and Opposition in

Exclusionary Bureaucratic-Authoritarian Regimes: The Situation in the 1980s," *Comparative Politics*, 17:1 (October):37-54

Evans, Peter. 1979. *Dependent-Development: The Alliance of Multinational, State, and Local Capital in Brazil*. Princeton: Princeton University Press

Fals-Borda, Orlando. 1970. "Formation and Deformation of Co-operative Policy in Latin America," International Institute for Labour Studies, *Bulletin* (June): 122-52

Feder, Ernest. 1971. *The Rape of the Peasantry: Latin American Landholding System*. New York: Anchor Books

— 1981. "Campesinistas y decampensinistas: Tres enfoques divergentes (no incompatibles) sobre la destrucción del campesinado," in *Desarrollo agrario y la América Latina*, Antonio García, ed., 199-225. México: Fondo de Cultura Económica

Fernández-Baca, Jorge, and Fabián Tume. 1981. "El complejo sectorial textil en el Perú," in *Producción algodonera e industria textil en el Perú*, Fernando Eguren et al., pp. 127-305. Lima: DESCO (Centro de Estudios y Promoción del Desarrollo)

Figueroa, Adolfo. 1977. "La economía rural en la Sierra peruana," in *Economía* (Pontificia Universidad Católica del Perú) 1 (December)

— 1980. "La economía campesina y su integración al mercado: el caso de la Sierra Sur del Perú," *Economía* (Pontificia Universidad Católica del Perú) 3:6 (December)

— 1982. "Restructuración agraria en la Sierra peruana," in *Situación actual y perspectivas del problema agrario en el Peru*, Fernando Eguren, ed., pp. 737-60. Lima: DESCO (Centro de Estudios y Promoción del Desarrollo)

Fitzgerald, E.V.K. 1979. *The Political Economy of Peru, 1956-1978: Economic Development and the Restructuring of Capital*. Cambridge: Cambridge University Press

— 1983. "State Capitalism in Peru: A Model of Economic Development and its Limitations," in *The Peruvian Experiment Reconsidered*, Cynthia McClintock and Abraham F. Lowenthal, eds., pp. 65-93. Princeton: Princeton University Press

Foxley, Alejandro. 1983. *Latin American Experiments in Neoconservative Economics*. Berkeley CA: University of California Press

Furtado, Celso. 1976. *Economic Development of Latin America: A Survey from Colonial Times to the Present*. Cambridge: Cambridge University Press

— 1987. "Transnationalization and Monetarism," *International Journal of Political Economy* 17:1 (Spring):75-87

Galli, Rosemary E. 1981. "Colombia: Rural Development as Social and Economic Control," in *The Political Economy of Rural Development: Peasants, International Capital and the State*, Rosemary E. Galli, ed., pp. 27-90. Albany: State University of New York Press

Garaycochea, Carlos. 1981. "Política financiera e industrialización," in *Estrate-*

gias y políticas de industrialización, pp. 277-97. Lima: DESCO (Centro de Estudios y Promoción del Desarrollo)

García, Antonio. 1973. *Sociología de la Reforma Agraria en América Latina*. Buenos Aires: Amorrortu

— 1976. *Las cooperatives agrarias en el desarrollo de América Latina*. Bogotá: Colatina

— 1981. "Naturaleza y limites de la modernización capitalista de la agricultura," in *Desarrollo agrario y la América Latina*, Antonio García, ed., pp. 9-35. México: Fondo de la Cultura Economica

García-Sayán, Diego. 1977. "La Reforma Agraria hoy," in *Estado y política agraria*, pp. 137-216. Lima: DESCO (Centro de Estudios y Promoción del Desarrollo)

González, Fernando. 1981. "Capital transnacional y políticas de industrialización," in *Estrategias y políticas de industrialización*, pp. 211-28. Lima: DESCO (Centro de Estudios y Promoción del Desarrollo)

Goodman, David, and Michael Redclift. 1981. *From Peasant to Proletarian: Capitalist Development and Agrarian Transition*. Oxford: Basil Blackwell

Grindle, Merilee S. 1986. *State and Countryside: Development Policy and Agrarian Politics in Latin America*. Baltimore MD: Johns Hopkins University Press

Hammergren, Linn A. 1977. "Corporatism in Latin America: A Reexamination of the 'Unique' Tradition," in *Comparative Politics* 9:4 (July):443-61

Harding, Colin. 1975. "Land Reform and Social Conflict in Peru," in *The Peruvian Experiment: Continuity and Change Under Military Rule*, Abraham F. Lowenthal, ed., pp. 220-53. Princeton: Princeton University Press

Hirschman, Albert O. 1979. "The Turn to Authoritarianism in Latin America and the Search for Its Economic Determinants," in *The New Authoritarianism in Latin America*, David Collier, ed., pp. 61-98. Princeton: Princeton University Press

Hopkins, Raul. 1981. *Desarrollo desigual y crisis de la agricultural peruana, 1944-1969*. Lima: IEP (Instituto de Estudios Peruanos)

Horton, Douglas. 1976. *Haciendas and Cooperatives: A Study of Estate Organization, Land Reform, and New Reform Enterprises in Peru*. Latin American Studies Program, Dissertation Series. Cornell University, Ithaca

ICA (International Cooperative Alliance). 1976. *Report of the ICA Commission on Co-operative Principles*. London

Instituto Nacional de Planificación. 1978. *La estructura agraria y el proceso de Reforma Agraria en el Perú*. Lima: Area de Planificación Social

IPEC (Instituto Peruano de Estudios Cooperativos. 1982. *Diagnóstico situacional del movimiento cooperativo peruano*. Lima

de Janvry, Alain, and Lynn Ground. 1978. "Types and Consequences of Land Reform in Latin America," *Latin American Perspectives* 5 (4 Fall): 90-112

de Janvry, Alain. 1981. *The Agrarian Question and Reformism in Latin America*. Baltimore MD: Johns Hopkins University Press

— 1984. "The Role of Land Reform in Economic Development: Policies and

Politics," in *Agricultural Development in the Third World*, Carl Eicher and John M. Staatz, eds., pp. 263-74. Baltimore, MD: Johns Hopkins University Press

Jereffy, Gary. 1983. *The Pharmaceutical Industry and Dependency in the Third World*. Princeton: Princeton University Press

Kaufman, Robert R. 1979. "Industrial Change and Authoritarian Rule in Latin America: A Concrete Review of the Bureaucratic-Authoritarian Model," in *The New Authoritarianism in Latin America*, David Collier, ed., pp. 165-253. Princeton: Princeton University Press

Kennworthy, E. 1970. "Coalitions in the Political Development of Latin America," in *The Study of Coalition Behavior*, S. Groennings, ed., pp. 103-40. New York: *Theoretical Perspectives and Cases from Four Continents*

Laclau, Ernesto. 1977a. "Feudalism and Capitalism in Latin America," in *Politics and Ideology in Marxist Theory*. London: Verso

— 1977b. "Towards a Theory of Populism," in *Politics and Ideology in Marxist Theory*. London: Verso

Lajo, Manuel. 1981. "La agroindustria y el sistema alimentario: diagnóstico y propuesta de reforma," in *Estrategias y politicas de industrializacion*, 335-70. Lima: DESCO (Centro de Estudios y Promoción del Desarrollo)

— 1982. "Política agraria y situación alimentaria," in *Situación actual y perspectivas del probema agrario en el Perú*, Fernando Eguren, ed., 177-94 Lima: DESCO (Centro de Estudios y Promoción del Desarrollo)

Lefeber, Louis, and Liisa L. North. 1980. "Introduction: Democracy and Development in Latin America," in *Democracy and Development in Latin America*, Louis Lefeber and Liisa L. North, eds., pp. 1-18. Toronto: CERLAC-LARU

Lele, Uma. 1981. "Co-operatives and the Poor: A Comparative Perspective," *World Development* 9, 55-72

Lehmann, David. 1978. "The Death of Land Reform: A Polemic," in *World Development* 6:3:339-45

Lipton, Michael. 1974. "Towards a Theory of Land Reform," in *Agrarian Reform and Agrarian Reformism: Studies of Peru, Chile, China, and India*, David Lehmann, ed. London: Faber and Faber

— 1977. *Why Poor People Stay Poor: Urban Bias in World Development*. Cambridge: Cambridge University Press

— 1984. "Urban Bias Revisited," in *Journal of Development Studies*. 20:3 (April):139-66

Malloy, James. 1974. "Authoritarianism, Corporatism and Mobilization in Peru," in *The New Corporatism: Social-Political Structures in The Iberian World*, Frederick B. Pike and Thomas Stritch, eds., pp. 52-84. Notre Dame IN: University of Notre Dame Press

— 1977. "Authoritarianism and Corporatism in Latin America: *The Modal Pattern*," in *Authoritarianism and Corporatism in Latin America*, James Malloy, ed., pp. 3-19. Pittsburgh: University of Pittsburgh Press

Martínez, Héctor. 1980. "Las empresas asociativas agrícolas peruanas," in *Realidad del campo peruano despues de la Reforma Agraria*, pp. 105-53. Lima: CIC

Martínez, Daniel, and Armando Tealdo. 1982. *El agro peruano 1970-1980: análisis y perspectivas*. Lima: CEDEP (Centro de Estudios para el Desarrollo y la Participación)

Matos Mar, José. 1976. *Yanakonaje y la Reforma Agraria*. Lima: IEP (Instituto de Estudios Peruanos)

Matos Mar, José et al. 1967. *La hacienda en el Perú*. Lima: IEP (Instituto de Estudios Peruanos)

Matos Mar, José, and José M. Mejía. 1980. *La Reforma Agraria en el Perú*. Lima: IEP (Instituto de Estudios Peruanos)

McClintock, Cynthia. 1981. *Peasant Cooperatives and Political Change in Peru*. Princeton: Princeton University Press

— 1982. "Post-Revolutionary Agrarian Politics in Peru," in *Post-Revolutionary Peru: The Politics of Transformation*, Stephen Gorman, ed., 135-56. Boulder CO: Westview Press

— 1983. "Velasco, Officers and Citizens," in *The Peruvian Experiment Reconsidered*, Cynthia McClintock and Abraham F. Lowenthal, eds., pp. 275-308. Princeton: Princeton University Press

Mejía, José Manuel. 1980. "De la Reforma Agraria a la promoción agropecuaria: un análisis crítico de la nueva política agraria," in *Promoción agraria: ¿Para quién?*, Jose M. Mejía, ed., pp. 10-40. Lima: Tiempo Presente

Mejía, Jose M., and Rosa Díaz. 1975. *Sindicalismo y la Reforma Agraria en el valle de Chancay*. Lima: IEP (Instituto de Estudios Peruanos)

Méndez, María Julia. 1982. "Las cooperativas agrarias de producción y las parcelaciones: situación actual y perspectivas," in *Situación actual y perspectivas del problema agrario peruano*, Fernando Eguren, ed., pp. 95-136. Lima: DESCO (Centro de Estudios y Promoción del Desarrollo)

Montoya, Rodrigo. 1974. *La SAIS Cahuíde y sus contradicciones*. Lima: Universidad de San Marcos. Mimeo

— 1978. *A propósito del caracter predominante capitalista de la economia peruana actual (1960-1970)*. Lima: Mosca Azul

— 1978. "Changes in Rural Class Structure under the Peruvian Agrarian Reform," in *Latin American Perspectives* 5(4):113-26

Moore, Mick. 1984. "Political Economy and the Rural-Urban Divide, 1767-1981," *Journal of Development Studies* 20:3 (April):5-27

North, Liisa L. 1981. "Political Conjunctures, Military Government and Agrarian Reform in Peru," in *Dependent Agricultural Development and Agrarian Reform in Latin America*, Lawrence R. Alschuler, ed., 103-33. Ottawa: University of Ottawa Press

O'Donnell, Guillermo A. 1973. *Modernization and Bureaucratic-Authoritarianism: Studies in South American Politics*. Berkeley CA: University of California, Institute of International Studies

— 1978. "Reflections on the Patterns of Change in the Bureaucratic-Authoritarian State," in *Latin American Research Review* 13:1:3-38

— 1979. "Tensions in the Bureaucratic-Authoritarian State and the Question of Democracy," in *The New Authoritarianism in Latin America*, David Collier, ed., pp. 285-318. Princeton: Princeton University Press

Paige, Jeffrey. 1975. *Agrarian Revolution: Social Movements and Export Agriculture in the Underdeveloped World*. New York: Free Press

Palmer, David Scott. 1973. *Revolution from Above: Military Government and Popular Participation in Peru, 1968-1972*. Diss., Ithaca NY: Cornell University

Palmer, David Scott, and Kevin Jay Middlebrook. 1976. "Corporatist Participation under Military Rule in Peru," in *Peruvian Nationalism: A Corporatist Revolution*, David Chaplin, ed., pp. 428-53. New Brunswick: Transaction Books

Pásara, Luís. 1978. "El proyecto de Velasco y la organización campesina," in *Apuntes* (Lima) 4 (8):59-80

Pearse, Andrew. 1975. *The Latin American Peasant*. London: Frank Cass

Pease, Henry. 1977a. "La Reforma Agraria peruana y la crisis del estado oligárquico," in *Estado y política agraria*, pp. 13-136. Lima: DESCO (Centro de Estudios y Promoción del Desarrollo)

— 1977b. *El ocaso del poder oligárquico: Lucha política en la escena oficial, 1968-1975*. Lima: DESCO (Centro de Estudios y Promoción del Desarrollo)

— 1981a. *Los caminos del poder: tres años de la crisis en la escena política*. Lima: DESCO (Centro de Estudios y Promoción del Desarrollo)

— 1981b. *A un ano del segundo belaundismo: un perfil del proceso político peruano*. Lima: DESCO (Centro de Estudios y Promoción del Desarrollo)

Peru. Ministerio de-Agricultura. 1982. *Estadística Agrícola* (Informativo 12, December). Lima: Oficina Sectoral de Estadística

Petras, James F. 1981. "The Latin American Agro-transformation from Above and Outside: The Social and Political Implications," in *Dependent Agricultural Development and Agrarian Reform in Latin America*, Lawrence R. Alschler, ed., pp. 29-47. Ottawa: University of Ottawa Press

Petras, James F., and A. Eugene Havens. 1981. "Peasant Movements and Social Change: Cooperatives in Peru," in *Class, State, and Power in the Third World*, James F. Petras with M. Morley et al., pp. 222-37. Montclair: Allanheld, Osmun

Portocarrero, Felipe. 1980. *Crisis y recuperación: economía peruana de los 70 a los 80*. Lima: Mosca Azul

Portocarrero, Filix. 1981. "Políticas de industrialización en el Perú," in *Estrategias y políticas de industrialización*, pp. 233-42. Lima: DESCO (Centro de Estudios y Promoción del Desarrollo)

Redclift, Michael R. 1978. *Agrarian Reform and Peasant Organization on the Ecuadorian Coast*. London: University of London Press

— 1984. "'Urban Bias' and Rural Poverty: A Latin American Perspective," in *Journal of Development Studies* 20 (3 April):123-38

Remmer, Karen, and Gilbert W. Merkx. 1982. "Bureaucratic Authoritarianism Revisited," in *Latin American Research Review* 17:2:3-40

Revesz, Bruno. 1980. "La Ley: ¿ promoción y desarrollo agrario?," in ¿ *Promoción agraria: Para quien?*, Jose M. Mejía, ed., pp. 41-62. Lima: Tiempo Presente

— 1982. *Estado, algodón y productores agrarios*. Piura: CIPCA (Centro de Investigación y Promoción del Campesinado)

Rubín, Emma. 1977. *Las CAP's de Piura y sus contradicciones*. Piura, Perú: CIPCA (Centro de Investigación y Promoción del Campesinado)

— 1978. *Que piensa el campesino de la Reforma Agraria?* Piura, Perú: CIPCA (Centro de Investigación y Promoción del Campesinado)

Salaverry, José. 1982. *El crédito agrario en el Perú*. Lima: Banco Central de Reserva

Sánchez, Rodrigo. 1981. *Tomas de tierra y conciencia política campesina*. Lima: IEP (Instituto de Estudios Peruanos)

Schmitter, Philippe C. 1974. "Still the Century of Corporatism?," in *The New Corporatism: Social-Political Structures in the Iberian World*, Frederick B. Pike and Thomas Stritch, eds., pp. 85-131. Notre Dame IN: University of Notre Dame Press

Schydlowsky, Daniel M., and Juan J. Wicht. 1983. "The Anatomy of Economic Failure," in *The Peruvian Experiment Reconsidered*, Cynthia McClintock and Abraham F. Lowenthal, eds., pp. 94-143. Princeton: Princeton University Press

Scurrah, Martin J., and Guadalupe Esteves. 1982. "The Condition of Organized labour," in *Post-Revolutionary Peru: The Politics of Transformation*, Stephen M. Gormen, ed., pp. 101-34. Boulder CO: Westview Press

Serra, Jose. 1979. "Three Mistaken Theses Regarding the Connection between Industrialization and Authoritarian Regimes," in *The New Authoritarianism in Latin America*, David Collier, ed., pp. 99-163. Princeton: Princeton University Press

Sheahan, John 1980. "Market-Oriented Economic Policies and Political Repression in Latin America," *Economic Development and Cultural Change* 28 (2):267-93

Stallings, Barbara. 1983. "International Capitalism and the Peruvian Military Government," in *The Peruvian Experiment Reconsidered*, Cynthia McClintock and Abraham R. Lowenthal, eds., pp. 144-80. Princeton: Princeton University Press

Stavenhagen, Rodolfo. 1975. *Social Classes in Agrarian Societies*. New York: Anchor Books

— 1981. "El campesinado y las estrategias del desarrollo rural," in *Desarrollo agrario y la América Latina*, Antonio García, ed., pp. 457-79. México: Fondo de la Cultural Economica

Stepan, Alfred. 1978. *The State and Society: Peru in Comparative Perspective*. Princeton: Princeton University Press

Bibliography 179

Strasma, John. 1976. "Agrarian Reform," in *Peruvian Nationalism: A Corporatist Revolution*, David Chaplin, ed., pp. 291-326. New Brunswick: Transaction Books

Sulmont, Denís. 1978. *Crisis, huelgas y movimientos populares urbanos en el Peru*. Lima: Pontificia Universidad Católica, Taller de Estudios Urbano-Industriales. Mimeo

— 1981. *La evolución reciente del movimiento sindical*. Lima: Pontificia Universidad Católica, Taller de Estudios Urbano-Industriales. Mimeo

Thorp, Rosemary. 1979. "The Stabilization Crisis in Peru, 1975-8," in *Inflation and Stabilization in Latin America*, Rosemary Thorp and Laurence Whitehead, eds., pp. 110-43. New York: Holmes and Meiers

— 1983. "The Evolution of Peru's Economy," in *The Peruvian Experiment Reconsidered*, Cynthia McClintock and Abraham F. Lowenthal, eds., pp. 39-61. Princeton: Princeton University Press

Thorp, Rosemary, and Jeoffrey Bertram. 1978. *Peru, 1890-1977: Growth and Policy in an Open Economy*. New York: Columbia University Press

Thorp, Rosemary, and Laurence Whitehead. 1979. "Introduction," in *Inflation and Stabilization in Latin America*, Rosemary Thorp and Laurence Whitehead, eds., pp. 1-22. New York: Holmes and Meiers

UNRISD (United Nations Research Institute for Social Development). 1969. *A Review of Rural Cooperation in Developing Areas*, by T.F. Carroll et al. Geneva

— 1971. *Cooperatives and Rural Development in Latin America: An Analytical Report*, by Orlando Fals-Borda. Geneva

— 1975. *Rural Cooperatives as an Agent of Change: A Research Report and Debate*. Geneva

Valderrama, Mariano. 1976. *Siete años de Reforma Agraria peruana*. Lima: Pontificia Universidad Católica del Perú

— 1982. "The Agrarian Reform: Continuity and Change in the Peruvian Rural Area," in *Rural Poverty and Agrarian Reform*, Steve Jones et al., eds., pp. 225-46. Dakar: Enda

Wallerstein, Michael 1980. "The Collapse of Democracy in Brazil: Its Economic Determinants," *Latin American Research Review* 15:3:3-40

Wiarda, Howard J. 1974a. "Social Change, Political Development and the Latin American Tradition," in *Politics and Social Change in Latin America: The Distinct Tradition*, Howard J. Wiarda, ed., pp. 3-22. Amherst: University of Massachusetts Press

— 1974b. "Corporatism and Development in the Iberii-Latin World: Persistent Strains and New Variations," in *The New Corporatism: Social-Political Structures in the Iberian World*, Frederick Pike and Thomas Stritch, eds., pp. 3-33. Notre Dame: University of Notre Dame Press

Wolf, Eric R., and Sidney W. Mintz. 1977. "Haciendas and Plantations," in *Haciendas and Plantations in Latin American History*, Robert G. Keith, ed., pp. 36-62. New York: Holmes and Meier

Wolfe, Marshall. 1984. "Participation: A View from Above," *CEPAL Review* 23 (August):155-79

Woy-Hazleton, Sandra L. 1982. "The Return of Partisan Politics in Peru," in *Post-Revolutionary Peru: The Politics of Transformation*, Stephen M. Gormen, ed., pp. 33-72. Boulder CO: Westview Press

Zaldívar, Ramon. 1974. "Agrarian Reform and Military Reformism in Peru," in *Agrarian Reform and Military Reformism: Studies of Peru, Chile, China, and India*, David Lehmann, ed., pp. 25-69. London: Faber and Faber

Index